STRONG

STRONG

Life, loss and eternal love for my daughter

ASHLEY CAIN

BLINK

bringing you closer

First published in the UK by Blink Publishing
an imprint of Bonnier Books UK
4th Floor, Victoria House
Bloomsbury Square
London WC1B 4DA
England

Owned by Bonnier Books
Sveavägen 56, Stockholm, Sweden

www.facebook.com/blinkpublishing
twitter.com/BlinkPublishing

First published in 2023 by Blink Publishing

Hardback ISBN: 978-1-78870-889-0
Trade paperback: 978-1-78870-940-8
Ebook ISBN: 978-1-78870-890-6
Audiobook ISBN: 978-1-78870-891-3

British Library Cataloguing-in-Publication Data:
A CIP catalogue record for this book is available from the British Library.

Design by www.envydesign.co.uk

Printed and bound in Great Britain by Clays Ltd, Elcograf S.p.A

1 3 5 7 9 10 8 6 4 2

Every reasonable effort has been made to trace copyright-holders of material reproduced in this book, but if any have been inadvertently overlooked the publishers would be glad to hear from them.

Blink Publishing is an imprint of Bonnier Books UK
www.bonnierbooks.co.uk

Beautiful, Strong, Courageous, Special.

My Champion, My Hero, My Guardian Angel,
My Daughter.

To the top of every mountain, to the bottom of
every valley, along every road, across every ocean –
I'll take you there, baby.

I will search the world, I will face its harms.

'Til I find my hero's welcome waiting in your arms.

I Love You, Champ

CONTENTS

Part One

AZAYLIA

CHAPTER 1

There was never any question of me failing. I'm not in the business of breaking promises – not to family, friends, or those good enough to support what I do.

Especially not to Azaylia.

What we did that day ended up being the most fulfilling, challenging and character-forming event since she passed away.

But man, it was hard.

I mean, it was hard.

It took place on the first anniversary of Azaylia's passing. Taking part were me, my brother, Matty, and my cousin, Tamika. Like everybody else in the family, Matty's incredible. His daughter, Anaya, was born around the same time as Azaylia. Tamika: again, she's next-level. Pure iron. A true Spartan. Together, the three of us planned to run from Nuneaton in Warwickshire to Trafalgar Square in London, the idea being that we set off on 23 April and ran overnight in order to arrive in London on the day of the anniversary, 24 April. We'd calculated it to be a distance of 100 miles over a period of twenty-four hours – an ultramarathon distance – but in fact it was 109 miles, and for a number of reasons it took us longer than twenty-four hours.

We had a support vehicle, friends in cars, fellow runners, a physio, a nutritionist and videographers. We had people joining us on bikes, including Azaylia's mum, Safiyya, and my sister, Alissia, and loads of well-wishers from the community, many of whom were also going to run with us. However, there would only be three runners doing the whole thing – me, Matty and Tamika.

I tend to mount these challenges at the toughest times, the big occasions: Azaylia's anniversary, her birthday, Childhood Cancer Awareness Month. I do them at these times because if I'm putting my body through pain then it reduces the hurt in my head and my heart, and also because it deflects from the fact that I can't do what other daddies do on these special days. I can't wake up my daughter on her birthday, plant a kiss on her face, make a fuss of her, spoil her rotten. So instead I give her a different kind of present. I take her on a journey. I show her great sights. I let her know that not only is she always in my thoughts and those of the whole family, but that she's also in the thoughts of the world.

For this journey I was taking her to Trafalgar Square, because that's where you find the lion statues, and Azaylia, who I used to call 'my lickle lion', was a lion in body, in spirit, in every sense of the word, and so I had to take her to see them.

And I was going to get her there, no matter what. As runners, all we knew was that we weren't going to quit.

Whether we had to run, walk or crawl, we were going to reach those lions. Yes, we wanted to do it in twenty-four hours, but mainly the goal was to complete it. After all, what kind of father promises his daughter a trip to the lions and then goes back on his word? Not me.

We started off with a private family get-together at Azaylia's resting place, Oaston Road Cemetery in Nuneaton. From there, it was a short walk to the official starting point, the Azaylia mural in Nuneaton town centre. Created by street artists n4t4, Wingy and Katie O, the mural features an image of Azaylia and has a *Lion King* theme. It also includes a compass and lines quoted from my eulogy to Azaylia: 'North to south, east to west, corner to corner, pillar to post ...'

I'll take you there.

As we arrived at the mural we saw that a crowd had already gathered to see us off. Among them was Billy Billingham, my instructor from the Channel 4 show I was on, *SAS: Who Dares Wins*, who'd driven three and a half hours to run the first five miles with us.

As we set off, we did so knowing that we'd done enough training beforehand. Although I'm a speed and power athlete I'd been priming for endurance with back-to-back runs, building confidence and stamina. Tamika and I had been doing regular thirty-mile runs, and on the basis of that alone I'd assumed we'd get to fifty, maybe sixty, miles of this ultramarathon quite comfortably.

But starting off that day it soon became apparent that whatever preparation we'd done would not be enough. Whether it was nerves, lack of sleep, pressure or something else, we started feeling the pain sooner than fifty or sixty miles.

Much sooner. Like six miles in was when it started to get hard. And by 'hard' I mean that I wasn't feeling the way I thought I should be feeling. I wasn't feeling great at all.

Fellow runners began to fall away. We had to say goodbye to Billy and others who'd joined us to pound the tarmac. Just us, the vehicles and the cyclists now. I never expected it to be easy. What was the point of doing it if it was going to be easy? I just hadn't expected it to get hard so quickly.

Our first checkpoint was Rugby, sixteen miles in. There, we were greeted by local people who wanted to wish us well, having heard about the run either through social or traditional media. We'd posted the route to let people know average times and were keeping them updated live as we were running. Social media gets a bad press, and as someone who's had his fair share of problems with it, I can vouch for the occasionally toxic atmosphere. But for something like this, it's absolutely fantastic. I'm telling you, there's no energy drink you can drink, no pill you can take, no words you can hear that give you the kind of lift you get when you literally see all of that support and feel all that love. They don't have to do it. That is the point. Everyone's got their lives to lead. Shopping to do. Meals to cook. Kids to collect from school. You name it. But instead of doing that, they give up their time, come out to see us, wish us well, lift us up. In football we always talk about the crowd being an extra man on the pitch. I'm here to tell you that it's exactly the same on an April day in Rugby in Warwickshire. Exactly the same.

We ate little jam doughnuts for energy and then set off again. That early problem already felt like ancient history. The doors of the support van were open, music was blaring, everybody in really high spirits, a great vibe. People pulled over in their cars to get out and run with us. We had the cyclists still. Morale was so high.

But, of course, the further we ran, the more the support dropped off. I was thinking, *sixteen miles, eighty-four to go*, knowing that things would only get harder.

And then, at thirty miles, my ankles went. They just *went*. My legs and feet have always been an issue with me. We'll get to it in more detail at some stage, but suffice to say I've had lots of operations for one reason or another.

This was bad, though. It felt as though my ankles had exploded, and as a result I could hardly walk, let alone run. If I stopped even just for the toilet, I couldn't walk after. I'd have to hobble, then walk and then slowly build up to a run in order to get going again.

This was something I definitely hadn't predicted. I could feel myself tensing, the fear rising, thinking, *I've got to finish this*.

Not finishing? Not an option.

But the pain. To be in so much pain at just thirty miles in.

The physio said stop. But I didn't stop, and nobody forced the issue. After all, everyone around me knew that stopping wasn't an option. They knew not to bring negativity to me. They knew that all I wanted from them was the will and knowhow to keep going.

I rang my dad at that point. My dad, well, he's old skool. 'You can do it – make it to 50 miles and it's all downhill from there,' he told me. And just the fact that my dad was saying that – I mean, it's rare to hear that kind of positivity from him. Maybe it gave me that extra bit of strength. In fact, it did.

And so, of course, I carried on.

CHAPTER 2

We kept on running. I was in agony at this point. Really quite serious pain. What spurred me on was thinking back to the cancer ward, remembering the kids who battle the most aggressive forms of leukaemia, who've had full bone-marrow transplants but wake up in the morning with smiles on their faces.

And what also spurred me on was thinking of Azaylia. How in eight months she taught me so much about life. Made me conscious to this world. And how with her passing, she took away one of the biggest fears I've ever had, which was my journey to the other side. Losing your daughter is something you'll never get over. It's something that'll haunt you forever. The injustice of it gnaws at your soul every single day. You realise on every birthday, Father's Day and Christmas that you're not going to be with her again. So instead you start to realise how much you can actually do. What your purpose is on this planet.

And that is enough for you not to stop. That's enough for you to run through the pain.

Fifty miles. We were chatting, trying to keep each other's spirits up. Each runner peaks and troughs at different points. You take a dip and the other two pick you up, the team chivvies you along.

I remember a checkpoint at Towcester. It felt like the whole town was outside, streaming out of the pubs, holding pints aloft and cheering us on.

Next was Milton Keynes. By this time we'd been running all day and we were well and truly drained. It wasn't just my ankle, we'd all picked up injuries. Not only that but we were mentally exhausted too. Incredibly, the support hardly seemed to falter, despite the darkness and the lateness of the hour.

I remember being in a car park late at night getting my ankle strapped, struggling to my feet and seeing phone lights before me, hearing people singing, 'Oobee-doo', from 'I Wan'na Be Like You', Azaylia's favourite song from *The Jungle Book*. I used to sing it to her when she was in hospital. As soon as I began that song, she'd smile. I'd asked the attendees to sing it at her funeral and now people sing it everywhere we go.

All but two of the cyclists had left us by this point, and a couple of my brother's mates joined us. We ran with a car in front and a car behind, seeing by the headlights. Sometimes the traffic wasn't getting past; we'd look back and see a tailback of forty cars. But you know what? People in the cars were fine. We didn't get any angry honking, drivers racing past and giving us the finger, nothing like that. People were into it. They knew what we were doing and they were giving it their support.

You'd have thought the night-time would be the toughest bit.

I mean, it was no picnic: we were soaking wet with sweat, it was freezing cold, and we were too tired to change clothes. Yet, on the other hand, the time seemed to go much more quickly.

We'd run past houses where people were waiting outside with their kids. This was at, like, 3 a.m. The night-time vibe brought out the music in people. I mean, we had guys setting up speakers on roundabouts. People blasting it out from passing cars. There was just something magical about the hours of darkness.

Then it started to get light again. We'd run about seventy miles by this stage and things began to get tougher. By which I mean, *even tougher*.

One of my friends, Shannon Courtenay, the boxer – I did *SAS: Who Dares Wins* with her – joined us. Although at this stage, I was not at my most sociable. For some deep-seated psychological reason – or maybe just the fact that I'd been running for twenty-two hours, most of it in excruciating pain – I was getting aggravated by things. Cars beeping were grinding my nerves. People cheering us on were, for some illogical reason, irritating me. I was in pain, I was wet and cold, and I was tired.

(But don't go getting the impression that I was ungrateful for the support. If you know me, you know that I'll stand and talk to supporters for as long as it takes. Anybody who gives their time to support the cause gets my minutes. But my emotions were up and down on that run. I was myself, but not really myself.)

Either way, I'm pleased to say that those feelings of irritation disappeared, and something amazing happened.

By now it was the morning of 24 April, the morning that Azaylia had passed just one year earlier.

And it hit me. At that exact moment of her passing twelve months previously, the emotion slammed into me all over again. I mean, I didn't know where I was, even the time. I hardly even knew my name, and yet suddenly there I was, back in that room, watching ...

It was like I'd had my soul ripped out again. Like she was reminding me: this is what you're doing and why.

Don't stop.

I cried. I let it all out. And then with Matty and Tamika's help, I gathered myself and I didn't stop, baby. I didn't stop, I kept going.

About eighty miles in we had a visit from adventurer and TV personality, Ant Middleton. Everybody went wild. I was on the floor stretching off when he arrived. Never met the guy before in my life, but he strode through everybody and gave me a kiss on my head, told me that how well I was doing. And he clearly had the key to my heart because he told me how amazing my daughter was; told me that she'd be proud of me.

After that he ran with us, and just his presence alone was enough to give the whole squad a lift, taking us from eighty miles to ninety – to within smelling distance of London, getting us close to those lions.

Ten miles to go now.

'Yo,' I said to our nutritionist. 'I need a pre-workout. I'm tired, I need a pre-workout.'

A pre-workout, if you don't know, is a hardcore drink that gives you energy before you exercise. Think Red Bull but turned up to the max.

The nutritionist wasn't sure. 'Mate, if you take it you're gonna go up but then you're gonna to come down.'

'It's time,' I insisted.

Thinking it was a good idea. Forgetting that it's a drink filled with caffeine, and what does caffeine make you want to do?

Shit.

As in, *Shit. I needed to go.*

I saw a hotel. Ducked inside. Got in a lift. Down some stairs. Found the toilet, did the business and then dashed (well, limped, hobbled) back outside to find that ...

Everybody had gone. Matty. Tamika. The support cars. Everybody.

Now, I like to think I'm a fairly distinctive dude. Difficult to lose in a crowd. But these guys had been up all night, probably half-hallucinating with fatigue. You could hardly blame them for not noticing my absence and carrying on without me.

Inside me though, some internal switch flipped. Abandoned and in a temporary state of shock, I'd been standing with my hands on my knees, shoulders heaving as I caught my breath, but now I stood up and I took off – and I swear to God, I ran quicker than I had for the whole twenty or so hours previously. That pre-workout drink was not just the cause of my problems, it was also the solution.

I hunted them down, joined up. And now we had three miles to go. Three miles. Just three miles, and then *bang*, my knee ligament went. I went from feeling the best I'd felt on the whole run, full of energy, to being in even more pain than I had been before. Pain everywhere. Trainers full of blood. Blisters everywhere. Blisters on blisters. Ankles swollen. Knee caving in.

And for a moment, I'll be honest, that felt like the last straw. Needing to take a seat, I dropped down to a low wall, feeling despondent. One hundred and six miles down, three miles to go, and that was it. We were finished. Done. My mind and body had disconnected. The body unable to obey the demands of the mind. It would not listen to the logic that said, *You only have three miles left.* We'd hurdled every physical and mental barrier so far. But not this one.

Side by side, the three of us sat on the wall, gathering ourselves. In our dark running gear and black gloves we looked like three exhausted cat burglars. Around us, people were telling us not to worry, we'd come so far, it didn't matter and so on. And I know they meant well, but it *did* matter. It did. I hadn't run 106 miles just to end it on a wall. None of us had.

We were there for five minutes or so. Five minutes was all it took to get ourselves together.

Come on, we're going to do this.

And we did.

We stood up and got moving. I was keeping my legs stiff, hardly running, doing a weird, shuffling Frankenstein walk for the last three miles to Trafalgar Square.

As we approached, the statues came into view and the end was in sight. Next, we saw the people: supporters, members of the team, my family. We had aimed to get there for midday, but as it turned out we didn't reach the square until six, and they had all waited for us, every one of them. I was exhausted, overcome.

As we arrived, after 109 miles and more than twenty-four hours of running, limping, hobbling, dragging ourselves from Nuneaton to London, I roared a lion roar.

And I called out her name.

CHAPTER 3

You might wonder why I do it. What drives me? The answer is a million reasons. And also just one. But let's start with three.

1. Because one thing that we've realised since starting
   The Azaylia Foundation is that diagnosis and treatment
   for childhood cancer is a broken system. Childhood
   cancer is the number-one killer of children aged one to
   nine in the UK, yet it receives less than 3 per cent of all
   cancer research funding. This is an absolute scandal,
   because if no money's going into the childhood-cancer
   space, then there'll be no new medical talent coming
   into that arena. How are these kids meant to survive
   and beat cancer if we don't have the talent, the research,
   the medication, the drugs, the treatment?

   So it's a broken system. Every penny I make on a

challenge goes into The Azaylia Foundation (and, yes, trolls, that's every fucking penny), where we use that money to help give kids treatment that they don't currently get under the NHS. We're all about changing the system, promoting early diagnosis and research into new treatment. We're about raising awareness of childhood cancer in a world that considers it to be rare, as a result of which we have this under-funding issue. We're committed to advancing early diagnosis and new treatment availability in the UK, while at the same time supporting children fighting cancer by helping them access treatment not covered by the NHS.

And that's what I do. I get up in the morning, and every minute that I'm not eating or in the bathroom (and sometimes then, too, not gonna lie), I'm working for the Foundation, either directly to raise money, or indirectly in order to raise its profile.

2. The second reason I do it is because by doing what I do, I can inspire others to be the best version of themselves. One of the many things driving me is a quote by a Greek philosopher, Heraclitus. I'm not going to pretend to be a student of Greek philosophy or even of Heraclitus, but this quote speaks to me. He says:

In battle, out of every one hundred men, ten shouldn't even be there. Eighty are just targets. Nine are the real fighters, and we are lucky to have them, for they make the battle. Ah, but the one, one is a warrior, and he will bring the others back.

And I think you know which one I am in that scenario.

3. I do it because at the age of seventeen I went to my nan's house during a period just after her sister's death when she'd stopped going to church. She hadn't stopped believing in God or being religious, just stopped attending church for reasons of her own. On that day she asked me where I was going, and for some reason – it was like the words were out of my mouth before I even had the chance to think of them – I said, 'Nan, we're going to church.'

   We went along together, and from there I started getting religion. These days my faith is strong – it's never ever been stronger than it is now. I won't lie, it was shaken when Azaylia passed. I couldn't help but question Him. I'd think, if there's a God, why am I watching kids go through so much pain? Why is my daughter having to fight this illness? How come you've even *got* an illness that kills kids? What's up with that?

   I still said my prayers. I still believed. But I asked my questions because I never understood why this could happen if there was a good Lord up there.

   Then, when she passed, I had to have a word with myself. I realised, *If I don't have my faith, I have nothing*. And I thought to myself that if I couldn't be sure that my daughter was in heaven, then there's no way that I can still be here on Earth; there's no way I could get up every single morning and fight, because – and this is the reason now, reason number three – I want to do enough while I'm still here on Earth that

I can guarantee my own place in heaven. To build my steps up when it's my final journey, so I can get up to the gates, and see her again. That's my selfish reason for doing what I do – so I can see Azaylia again, in heaven.

So that's three reasons. But like I say, there are a million others too. I do what I do for the kid in hospital who needs our help. I do it because I have a need to do something good with my days. To show up and fight. Because I connect with her most when I'm feeling the most pain, and so I get to feel that I'm spending time with her, doing the things with her that I was never able to do when she was alive because her life was spent lying in a hospital bed. I do it because I'm inspiring people to know that no matter what you've been through, if you're prepared to fight you can rise above it, you can overcome any adversity. I do it out of a need to face down the dark. A need to take a mindset and turn it into action. A need to keep on learning and developing as a person. A need to push myself, get into beast mode and *go*.

But at the end of the day, the million reasons boil down to just one reason. The only reason.

Azaylia.

CHAPTER 4

Before I go on to talk about Azaylia, I should say that her mother and I are no longer together. Safiyya and I still share a living space, we care for each other very much, and we work together for The Azaylia Foundation – in terms of the way we function, very little has changed – just that we're no longer in a romantic relationship. A loving relationship, yes. A deep, mutually respectful relationship built on the foundations of what we've endured together. Absolutely. Just not a romantic one.

Back in 2019 we were very much a couple, though, little knowing the trials that lay ahead. Back then I was still riding the crest of the reality-TV star wave – more of which later – as well as running my own clothing brand and, I have to say, doing pretty well. For the first time in my life, I felt like I was … I don't know if 'stable' is the right word, but something like that. I was living with a woman I loved. I was doing all right financially. When you have all that you begin to wonder what it might be like to raise a family.

So the idea came from me, Saf being a bit more reticent on the matter. It wasn't that she hands down didn't want a baby, just that she wasn't sure. Maybe she didn't see in herself what I saw, which was the nurturing and caring side to her. She's somebody who wants to look after you. Like if she's around the family, she wants to cook, she wants to see that everyone's looked after. In her I saw a strong person and a carer. I saw great mum material.

For a while we tried with no success, to the point where we ended up going to the doctor's to see if there was anything wrong with us. Nope. Everything in working order. We kept on trying, until one day I was on my way home and, on a whim, stopped off at Boots and bought a test. It was no more than that, just a feeling I had.

'Yo, do you need a wee?' I called, the first words out of my mouth as I barrelled through the door to our apartment, brandishing the box.

Saf was like, 'What's up with you?' but she knew me well enough to know that when I get a feeling I have to act on it. And anyway, she needed a wee, so duly trudged off to the bathroom to do the honours.

And I remember having the pregnancy test in my hand. I remember staring at it, just waiting for the result to appear.

Waiting.

Until ...

Positive.

I had a drink that night. Saf sat on the sofa and watched me dance around the room, celebrating.

'I'm not going to drink,' she announced. 'I'm pregnant.'

And we looked at each other, hardly able to believe the words out of her mouth were real. *'I'm pregnant.'*

She's pregnant. Saf is pregnant. She's going to be a mum and I'm going to be a dad.

I was like, 'Oh my God, I need to tell someone.'

'No,' she almost yelled. 'You can't, you can't.'

And she was right because you're not supposed to tell anyone. Not until you're at least twelve weeks gone and you've had the scan.

But oh, man, that was hard. I was the most excited I've ever been about anything and I couldn't tell anyone. Not even my mum, and I'm *really* close to my mum. So that was a new feeling: absolute frustration.

But there was another one, too. Anxiety. The feeling that Saf had a tiny little seed trying to sprout root inside her. The fear that sometimes those seeds don't take root and a miscarriage can happen.

But I played my part and kept schtum for twelve weeks, after which we had the scan. The scan was good, and I told practically everyone in the world: friends, family, colleagues, anyone who'd listen.

The family was electrified, of course. Mum, who wanted nothing more than to be a grandma, was over the moon, as was Saf's mum, who needed to be sure that I had everything under control; that I could support my new family. I assured her I could. I told her that my only focus from now on was Saf and the baby. My only focus. And I'd never been more sure of anything in my life.

I called my brother, Matty. 'Yo, I've got something to tell you, bro, you're going to be an uncle again.'

And he went, 'Yeah, bro, so are you.'

No way! What's more, it turned out that our due dates were literally days apart.

'You're going to have a boy, I know you are,' he said. We both wanted boys. 'I know it, bro. You're going to have a boy.'

From then on we'd be talking about it all the time, winding each other up. Even so, we made a pact to wait and share the sex of our kids together.

Next it came to the big twenty-week scan, the one where they tell you whether you're having a boy or a girl. Driving to the clinic, we were two minutes away when I saw a pink balloon bobble across the road. And something you have to know about me is that I'm big on signs. Like if I'm sent a sign, I'll take it, and this one couldn't have been more plain: we were going to have a girl.

We're going to have a girl and she's going to break my heart. That's all I was thinking. That was it. *We're having a little girl. I'm going to love this little girl. She's going to be a daddy's girl, but she's going to break my heart.*

And sure enough, they confirmed it inside. We were going to have a beautiful little girl.

Later, I phoned Matty for the big reveal.

'Bro, I'm having a girl,' I announced.

'So am I,' he said, and we laughed and got to planning daddy-daughter days, all the stuff we were going to do, and it felt absolutely amazing; I felt like I was giving the greatest present to my family and to myself. I felt like I was beginning a process of shedding old skin, becoming a new man.

After that, I started getting up at 4 a.m. every day, working harder than I'd ever worked before.

Two reasons: firstly, I wanted to feather the nest, make sure we had plenty of money for when the baby came; secondly, I wanted to make sure I could spend as much time as possible with Saf and our baby after the birth. I'd already decided what sort of dad I wanted to be. One who was present. Who was there.

CHAPTER 5

Covid kicked off when Saf was pregnant, just after we'd moved into a new place in Nuneaton. It would have taken more than that to take the wind out of our sails, though. We were busy preparing, building a home for our new arrival, giddy as kids with it all.

When it came to naming her, I said to Saf, 'She's got to be one of the A's,' because I'm Ashley, my dad's Anthony, my sister's Alissia ... there are so many A's in our family, and I wanted to stay true to that tradition. So Saf and I decided to come up with a bunch of names each and then compare notes – except we didn't come up with a bunch of names, we came up with one each, and they were both Azaylia. At the time, we both just loved the name for our own reasons, but recently we found out that it means 'reserved by God'. It sent both a shiver down my spine and a tear down my cheek.

As for Azaylia's middle name, that came courtesy of my

grandma, Cynthia (who sadly passed away in 2022, while I was filming *SAS: Who Dares Wins*). She was a Cain, but her maiden name was Diamond. That side of the family is from Saint Vincent, home to a massive family of Diamonds, and the more I thought about it, the more fitting it was for Azaylia. Diamond: a beautiful stone but one of the toughest materials on Earth. Dazzling but strong.

I hadn't met Azaylia yet, but I knew.

Saf pretty much agreed when it came to the name. No, I tell a lie. There was a tussle when I put forward 'Azaylia Lion Cain', and she was like, 'She's a girl, she can't be Lion,' and I was all, 'But, Saf, she's going to be a lion, I know it.'

Either way, we changed direction and when it came to Azaylia Diamond Cain we spoke with one voice.

Saf was an absolute legend during pregnancy. She really held it down. She kept active, stayed focused, never complained. The closer it got to the due date, the more I thought, *You got this.*

And then one day, her waters broke.

Our new house was three minutes away from George Eliot Hospital in Nuneaton, and that's where we went. It being Covid, numbers were restricted, but there was no way I was going to miss the birth. Luckily, we had a ground-floor room with a window, so certain members of the family were able to gather outside: my mum, my sister, Saf's mum, all of them at the window, which was ajar.

Saf had asked me to create a playlist, which I called *Oh Shit, It's That Time*. It included 'Fantasy' by Mariah Carey, 'You Rock My World' by Michael Jackson, 'Love Like This' by Faith Evans and loads more, so that went on. I remember getting McDonald's dropped off. I was dancing around, trying to keep her spirits up, the grans-to-be outside calling encouragement through the window. We were rocking that room.

But there was a problem. Saf was in a lot of pain resulting from the fact that Azaylia had turned in the womb. Mother and baby were spine to spine, which is bad, really bad. Nurses dressed in Covid-safe protective clothing bustled around busily, a mood of slight concern in the room now. Saf and I sampled the gas and air.

Saf had always wanted a natural birth, but the more pain she was in, the less likely it seemed that she'd get her wish. I stayed with her, sitting on the bed, chatting rubbish, trying to distract her from the pain. If I moved – if even for a second she couldn't see me – she'd cry out for me, 'Ash? Ash? Where are you?' and I'd have to scuttle back, take her hand, reassure her that I was close by.

'You got this, Saf,' I kept telling her. 'You got this.'

I was there for hours and hours, hunched over the bed, my back was killing me even as I was painfully aware that my own discomfort was but a tiny, tiny fraction of what Saf was going through.

They made a decision: Saf would have to have an epidural and Caesarean. By the time they gave her the epidural she'd had so much gas and air, it was like she was drunk. She wasn't listening to anybody, so I had to step in and go, 'Look, Saf, they want this to go down now. Come on, let's do it. It's going to be all right. You've done all you could and you're going to have a little scar, but that little scar's a war wound of you birthing the most amazing thing that you or me are ever going to have. So you be proud of that scar.'

Next, she was called in to have a Caesarean. I had to wait

outside so they could prepare her, but she wasn't really hearing what she was being told. She was still crying out for me. I could hear her yelling, 'Where's Ashley? Where's Ashley?' with the nurses saying to her, 'Calm down. You've got to calm down or he can't come in.'

She did, and I was allowed back in. By this time I'd stopped with all the dancing and joking and was just there to be her rock, holding her hand in the operating theatre, thinking, *You're amazing*. Any bloke who's been through childbirth with his partner will tell you the same: you spend the whole time slack-jawed with admiration that any human being can withstand such agony. That was how I felt about Saf then; how tough she was.

As Azaylia entered this world – at 6.56 a.m. on 10 August 2020 – Saf's first words were, 'Ashley's got to cut the cord. Ashley, you cut the cord,' absolutely insistent, not wanting to risk anybody else doing it. To be honest, I was more focused on looking after her and wanting to see Azaylia, but I did as asked, looking at our newborn baby, thinking how tiny she was, how precious.

I remember saying to the nurses, 'Can I kiss her?'.

'Sure, Dad, you can give your little girl a kiss, she's yours.'

Nurses look like angels at times like that. As though they're bathed in light.

So I picked up Azaylia. I held our little baby, and I kissed her, and a feeling swept through me like an emotional tidal wave, unlike anything I'd ever felt before. A mix of love and fear and a vast, almost overwhelming sense of responsibility. If you're a parent, you'll know what I mean.

My next impulse was to take her to Saf. *You've done*

this, I was thinking. *You can't miss out on this*, and the next thing you know, I was handing Azaylia to Saf, which was an incredible feeling. Like I was the first person ever to hand a baby to her mother. A feeling like this gesture was the most important of my life, everything I'd ever done was leading up to that moment.

And what's weird is that things only seemed to intensify from there. For a start I had a steep learning curve in baby care. Having had a C-section, Saf was completely bed-bound, almost totally immobile. And it struck me that I knew nothing about looking after babies. Zilch. Zero. Nothing. Nada.

I was thinking, *I don't know what to do. I've got to change a nappy. I don't want to hurt her, I don't want to make her cry, I just want to be able to do it right.*

'You'll be alright,' Saf was telling me, and of course she was right, and in fact it turned out that I was the first person to change Azaylia's nappy, which I think in many ways was important, going forward. I didn't know how to do it, so I had to get it sorted quick, and that prepared us for the rest of our journey. It gave me an immediate introduction to that kind of hands-on fathering that I was aiming for anyway.

Because it was Covid, I had to leave the hospital. It was a long two days before mother and daughter came home and we had Azaylia in a crib next to our bed. If it was during the night and Azaylia woke up, I'd get up and do the running around so Saf could feed her. I had no choice but to be in charge of all the mundane household tasks – we'd been told that it would take Saf twelve weeks to recover from her Caesarean – but I loved it anyway. I loved my newfound job of keeping house, but mainly I loved looking after Azaylia.

As any new parent knows, all your focus goes there. Your world shrinks to the four walls of your home, the bedroom, the cot within it and the baby swaddled in the crib. For the first time in your adult life you literally have one job and that job is to take care of this beautiful baby.

I couldn't stop worrying, though. If Azaylia was in the bed, I'd be terrified of accidentally rolling onto her. I was a big bloke back then, probably about 17 stone. If I so much as dropped an arm on her …

It didn't bear thinking about. Saf would take the piss out of me. According to her, I was a panicky parent. And maybe I was. But that was my focus. I had one job, and it was to make sure this little girl stayed safe. I'd spend hours kissing her, just gazing at her. I used to kid myself that she was smiling at me.

'It's probably just wind,' Saf would say.

We had guests too, of course. We could hardly get rid of our two mums, who were almost as excited as we were about having a new baby around. Again, Covid made it difficult, but the lockdown restrictions had eased by then, and we managed a way around it, bending but not breaking the rules.

The guys came, too. My dad, various uncles and, of course my brother, Matty. Anaya had been born a couple of days before Azaylia, so Matty brought her over for the two to meet. There's a photograph of us, both holding our girls, and I remember so vividly how for the first time in my life I felt … *content*. As though I previously had no identity, but now I did. I was a dad. A daddy.

This is it, I thought. *This is my next chapter.*

Part Two
GOING PRO

CHAPTER 6

I grew up in Bedworth, Warwickshire. My mum, Vicky, is white British, whereas my dad, Anthony, is black Caribbean, born in Britain but with roots in Saint Vincent – home to many, many Diamond and Cain family members.

Mum and Dad split up in about 2017. That's life. These things happen. But they were together during my childhood, plus we had relatives nearby, so I got to spend time with most of my extended family. I was a cheeky little sporty kid, friendly, with plenty of love in my heart, and I spent loads of time round their houses or being taken by them to training and football games.

But home was home and 5, Joseph Luckman Road in Bedworth was the house that I shared with my mum and dad and my younger sister, Alissia.

Mum? What can you say about my mum? One of life's carers, she's literally lost if she's not got something to do for somebody. Being a grandma completed her, and she was utterly broken when Azaylia passed. As for me, growing up, she was just a great mum. I always knew that whatever happened, she had my back.

Dad was a different proposition. He had something of a colourful past. If you want to know just how colourful, let's put it this way: all my siblings have different mums apart from me and Alissia. There's Ryan, the oldest, then Matty, then me, then Chelsea, then Alissia. So, a lot of kids, a lot of mums. That was Dad.

And I say this without comment or judgement, because Dad was (and still is) a great father. He was a tough guy – a man who had been forged in steel by what was a fairly tough upbringing (Grandma and Grandad Cain, his parents, were always lovely to me, but I'd hear the stories, and I knew that Grandad Cain had the devil in him, right up until the day he died ...). And I know that Dad never wanted to subject me to the upbringing he'd had, just as I, when Azaylia was born, wanted to fine-tune the good things from my dad and perhaps filter in some of the stuff that I felt I'd missed out on. Like I say, not his fault. Totally to do with his environment, his culture, his upbringing, but he wasn't the most affectionate. That's the way he was.

By day, Dad worked in an engineering factory. By night, he was a bouncer, and it was that second occupation that made him notorious where I grew up. He never raised a hand to anyone in our family – quite the reverse, he looked after us all, and in particular always, *always* looked after his kids – but there was no doubt about it, he was a hard man. I remember one time him coming in with his nose literally hanging off, like someone had taken an axe to it, my uncle trying to hold his nose onto his face, and a lot of blood.

So, yes, he was no stranger to that world. Practically lived there. But go into the local pubs and you wouldn't hear that Anthony Cain was a nutter or a psycho. You'd hear that he was a hard man who'd beat you down if you got out of line. But a man of honour. A fair man. A man who commanded respect.

Some of that strength rubbed off on me, I guess. I'm not as tough as him – at sixty he still works out, is as fit as they come, could take on the best of us if it came to it – but I'm tough enough, and I've had my crazy times. However, there's a real caring and affectionate side to me that 100 per cent comes from my mum and from her side of the family. I've had to literally drag that side of things over to my dad. It's only recently that me and my dad started shaking hands and hugging.

So home life was good. School, on the other hand? That was a different matter. I was a clever kid, but I always used to get in trouble. It wasn't like I was bad, just a bit naughty – a lovable rogue, if you like.

My trouble was that I always needed to know the pathway. You can't tell me to do something and expect me to do it without telling me why. Give me a good reason why I should be doing it, I'll do it all day long. If you go, 'Do that,' and I go, 'Why?' and you say, 'Because I said so,' then that's not good enough. At school, well, sometimes you get a reason, sometimes you don't. So sometimes I'd do as I was told and sometimes I wouldn't.

(Incidentally, it was another of those things that I planned to put right with Azaylia, if only I'd been given the chance.

I always wanted her to know the pathway. I wanted her to appreciate the reasoning behind every decision.)

So that was me, at school. Not exactly academic, but fairly bright. Not exactly the best-behaved kid in the class, not by a long chalk. But certainly not the worst. And yet I stood out. I stood out for two reasons. Firstly, sport, a subject to which I'll return. Secondly, my ethnicity.

CHAPTER 7

Bedworth wasn't exactly the most multicultural place in the world; in fact, I think I was one of just two mixed-race kids in the whole of my infant school and then again in junior school. At senior school there were three mixed-race kids out of 1,800 and one black kid who joined in the last year. Like I said, not exactly a vibrant cultural melting pot.

I'm trying to remember how old I was when I first heard it. And even what it was. But it started – I'm pretty sure it was in junior school – and once it had started, like the proverbial snowball, it just kept on getting bigger.

'P**i', that was one of them. Offensive and inaccurate. 'Black bastard.' Racists tend to like the way the two Bs go together. 'Ni**er', of course.

If the words offend you, I apologise. As you may or may not know, they're even more offensive when you're on the receiving end.

I remember one kid wanted to fight me after school. I recall very clearly being utterly confused as to *why* he wanted to fight me and knowing now, of course, that the simple reason was that he hated me for the colour of my skin. We tussled. I remember that. I remember another incident when my sister met me out of school, an older kid said something, and we had a scuffle.

But junior school was nothing compared to senior school. Outside of school I hung around with the younger members of my family, most of whom were or mixed race. The kids I played football with were black or mixed race. They had that black culture in them.

That was evenings and weekends, however. The rest of the time I was going to school in an area where you never saw black people. Educationally, I was in all the top sets. I got top grades, not necessarily because I was doing all my homework and being especially studious, just because I was naturally quite clever. School could – and should – have been good for me, if not for the abuse.

You might wonder why I don't call it bullying. Bullying makes it seem like I was a victim, but I would never choose to look at it that way. I don't like anything that victimises me, because fundamentally that experience moulded me, it made me a lot stronger. It made me realise that there were hurdles in life and that I could cope with them.

And the weird thing was that in actual fact I was quite popular at school. I had plenty of mates and girls liked me. Just that there was a section – mainly older kids who had already left school – who took against me and did so on the basis of my ethnicity.

Even so, at the time, I'm not gonna lie, it was hard. I was a thirteen-year-old kid and I'd reach the end of school every day, put my trainers on and make a decision: front or back gate? Because I knew that kids would be waiting for me. Kids would turn up in their cars just to try and meet me out of school.

I remember going into town – about the same age, thirteen – and six lads, all of whom were older, had left school, jumped me. No one helped. Everyone was laughing, and I got attacked. I knew it was just because they had hatred and discrimination in their hearts.

I would go home to my nan's house – my mum and dad being at work – but I didn't tell them what I was going through. I didn't subject them to that. So, I just used to keep it to myself. Even after that time I got beaten up in town I just told them that I'd got roughed up playing football.

I used to fight, sometimes, but most of the time I was too busy trying to get away. Knowing that I was being targeted for the colour of my skin. For the fact that I wore the clothes of my culture.

It carried on until one day when I was in Year 9 or 10, something inside me snapped. I thought, *You know what? I don't want this, I don't deserve this shit.* So I rang up my brothers, Ryan and Matty. I called my cousins too. And I told all of them what was going on. I told them that I was being targeted and that I'd been targeted for years, and that I didn't want to run any more.

I walked out the gate that day and instead of the racists I had my people there to greet me, an army of them, and together we took the long way home from school, a mini-march of our own. We caught a few of the racists in town that day, and let's just say that I got a little payback.

You might wonder if I regret taking so long to call for back-up. Answer: no, I don't regret it, because as I said, I built up a resilience during that time. It made me strong.

CHAPTER 8

said that me being mixed race wasn't the only reason I stood out at school. There was also the fact that I used to get a lot of attention from the girls – hey, I'm only saying, just speaking facts here – while another reason was sport. I was really, really good at sport.

For a start, I was competitive – still am – which you might say is a basic requirement for being good at sport. Secondly, I was strong and powerful. Even as a little kid, I was never a 'little' kid. I had shoulders and abs, which meant that I could take you on, and if I took you on, I'd usually win. Thirdly, and probably most important for me going forward, I was quick. Very quick. I mean, every sports day at every school I ever attended, I was the quickest. And that speed would go on to provide the foundation of everything I went on to do.

Which was? Actually, at first I was into horse-riding, would you believe? But then it was kind of decided that I should try my hand at football, with my dad and grandad especially keen that I should give it a go. Living over the road from my nan's were two guys I knew from school – twins who were my best mates in infant and junior school – who invited me to play football at Bedworth.

And even though I wasn't quite the football-mad kid you might have expected me to be, and only really went because other people wanted me to try it, I actually turned out to be quite good at it. It wasn't like I had exceptional football skills, just that I was quicker and stronger than everyone else, and playing up front where I could run at defenders was enough to make me top scorer in the league for every year that I played.

At eight or nine I was spotted by Leicester City; at ten I had all the local academies knocking on my door: Coventry, Leicester, Villa, Birmingham, Wolverhampton and West Brom. Coventry were nearest and they were in the Premiership and had a good academy, so I chose them.

(My team, by the way, were Manchester United. The first game I ever saw was at Highfield Road, watching Coventry City play Man U, a time when the likes of Giggs, Cole and Beckham were playing for United. Even though they were beaten 3-2 by Coventry that day, Man U were the glamour side. And from that moment on, they were the team I supported.)

Meanwhile, I had started doing athletics and was winning at county and then at national levels. At Cov, I stood out and scored loads of goals. All this while still at secondary school.

By now my life was dominated by football. I had training Monday, Wednesday and Friday nights. I was athletics training Tuesday and Thursday evenings, playing matches for Cov on Saturdays and in athletics competitions on Sundays.

Did I mention that my grandad was my willing chauffeur during this time? If not, then here it is. Props to him for driving me around, standing on the touchline and cheering me on.

I played on the wing or upfront. At that age my favourite player was Ronaldo – the original Brazilian Ronaldo. I loved the flair of the Brazilians. I loved watching players who could get the ball and lift you off your seat, and I felt like I could do that myself, playing up front or on the wing. I'd get the ball and haunt the defence. Parents watching would get excited when the play came my way. I'd give my full-back nightmares every single time. The reason was that I had power and pace. I could run the full length of the pitch at pace without getting tired.

Oh, and guess what happened next? I only got a call-up for England.

CHAPTER 9

The call-up was for England U14s, which meant that I had to travel to the England training camp for pre-match preparations for a game against Turkey.

Writing that now, it's just another sentence, and not the monumental event it was at the time, but back then, it was immense. Absolutely immense. Me, a kid from Nuneaton playing for Coventry was good, but a kid from Nuneaton who played for Coventry who had also been called up for England? That was better than good. That was off-the-scale good.

My dad was someone who also said it like it was. He pushed me to be the best that I could be. I understand that now, even if I didn't at the time. He was impressed with the England call-up. To him it would have been the first step on my way to fulfilling my potential, and that's all he ever wanted for me.

So there I was, training with England at Coventry City's

first-team training ground, about two days before the game, this was. I was running, nobody near me at the time, when suddenly …

Bang.

This incredible pain in my groin, as though somebody had kicked me in the balls. I dropped to the floor, literally in excruciating pain.

Now, for some reason, there were no medical staff able to diagnose the problem at the Sky Blue Lodge. I was in that much pain, not to mention gutted that my time there had come to a premature and agonising halt that I don't really recall the sequence of events. It was just that one minute I was on the deck, in pain, holding my balls, the next my dad was turning up to take me home.

'We need to get you to a hospital,' he told me.

I refused. I wanted to be at home in bed. The initial pain, which had been like somebody had let off a firework in my pants – and I'm not even joking – had slightly subsided, leaving behind it a terrible, throbbing ache. At home I crawled into bed with a hot water bottle clasped to my groin.

'You need to go to the doctor's or a hospital,' said my mum, echoing my dad's words.

'No, I'm not going,' I insisted.

I spent the day in bed. Then the next day, with me still in pain, Mum used her nuclear option: 'If you don't want to go to the doctor's, you're going to school.'

I called her bluff and went to school, still in severe pain and clearly in no fit state to be there.

'What are you doing in school?' asked one of my teachers as I tried to skulk past in the corridor.

'Because my mum said I've got to,' I told him through gritted teeth.

'No way. Look at you. You can't be in here.'

They rang my mum, who picked me up. 'Right,' she said, no-nonsense, 'you're going to the doctor's.'

The doctor commenced his examination with a question that no fourteen-year-old ladies' man wants to hear: 'Have you ever had sexual intercourse?'

My mum was in the room. I was thinking, *God, why is he asking me this?* The thing was that I'd always been quite popular with girls. I'd started early.

'Yes,' I admitted sheepishly.

'When was the last time?'

'Last week.'

After all that, the upshot was that I had to go to the hospital anyway. And if you want to know the definition of awkward silence, it's the silence between a mother and her son who's just admitted that he's sexually active at fourteen as they make the journey from the doctor's to the hospital in order to find out what's wrong with his bits. The pain in my poor bollocks was bad but it was nowhere near as excruciating as that silence.

At the hospital, *finally*, I was diagnosed. I had a torsion. A twisted testicle that led fairly swiftly to an operation, the end result of which was that I lost the testicle.

And what did that mean for me, growing up? I'm not entirely sure, is the answer. I've never really gone into it further than asking the odd question, but what I will say is that at fourteen, I was bigger than everyone. But after that, I didn't grow at all, and I've often wondered if that was why. The fact that I had lost one testicle and taken a bit of damage to the other one was something that mentally played on me. Possibly it held me back in terms of my growth. Certainly, it meant that I had to have a lot of time off school and off football.

Everything looked and worked fine. But it was a mad, bad time and something that lived with me for a long while afterwards. I had my chance of an England cap snatched away from me. I constantly worried about my development. It was a harsh but early lesson to learn, but something that would clearly help me well into the future. I just didn't realise it yet.

In the meantime, my footballing career kept chugging away.

CHAPTER 10

And I loved the game. I loved competing. I thrived off being up against somebody and coming off best. I loved being quicker, stronger, fitter. I literally lived for winning.

These days I'm so much more humble, but back then you wouldn't find anybody more competitive than me. Pretty soon, I was playing in one or two age groups above my own, while in athletics I used to train with international sprinters, training so hard that I used to throw up on the track. That's how much I wanted to win.

Looking back now, I can see that this hunger came partly from within and partly from my long-suffering grandad, from whom I used to get a real sense of belief. To him I was the golden boy, the best in the world. 'Well done, congratulations, so proud of you.' That's what I had from him and from that side of the family.

It also came from my father's side of the family, from whom it was more a case of me needing to prove myself to them. And somehow within me those two ideologies smushed together to make this ultra-competitive little kid.

Funny, my dad used to say to me, 'The problem with you is that you don't love football,' which seemed odd given that I was with Coventry. It's difficult to know what more he expected of me. And yet …

He was right.

Having been there at the beginning, giving me a gentle shove in the direction of football, he had realised that my gift, such as it was, lay not with one particular sport, but with sport in general. I just loved to compete. And, sure, I liked football, but he was right, I didn't *love* it. I didn't live and breathe it. It wasn't a matter of life and death to me. I hardly ever watched *Match of the Day*, for example. I wouldn't be interested in transfers or manager news. I liked watching goals, skills and tricks and I liked playing the *FIFA* videogame, but I was never one for sitting down to watch football.

'That's your trouble,' he said to me. 'You don't want it enough.'

He thought I should pursue athletics as well as continuing with my education. He knew what I would soon learn, which was that I'd see four or five kids getting dropped every single year, their hopes of stardom dashed, their long-held dreams of becoming a pro reduced to pieces on the floor.

The thing is that football is a game of opinion. It's not like athletics, where the clock dictates your skill. In football – and I've had it several times – you can be at a club with a manager who loves you, only for a new manager to arrive, and you don't get on with them so well, so they leave you out of the squad, you stop getting games, you lose confidence and so on and so forth until you're locked into a vicious circle.

Anyway, although I'd been accepted into college on a business and economics course after my GCSEs, Coventry City swooped in and offered me a scholarship. They wanted me to spend most of the week training with them, as well as doing one and a half days a week at college, studying for a BTEC in sports.

And so, in 2005, I left school at fifteen and went into a full-time apprenticeship with Coventry City. By this time, I knew – or at least I thought – that whatever happened, sport would be my career. Yes, I listened when my dad said I should pursue athletics, but the fact was that Coventry came in for me. They were willing to pay me to play football, and show me a kid who would resist that. Go on. I'll wait.

So now I was on a two-year YTS at Sky Blue Lodge with Cov, doing all the stuff you might expect: cleaning the first-team boots, looking after the kit and so on, as well as training in the mornings and the afternoons, on Wednesdays doing a full day at college, and then playing on Saturdays.

Now, leading up to the beginning of my apprenticeship, we had two academy directors, Steve Ogrizovic and Brian Burrows, both of whom were proper old school Coventry legends who didn't take any shit – men's men through and through. A lot were terrified of them, and with good reason – they could be terrifying – but I used to like them, mainly because they called it how they saw it; they made their judgements for good, sound footballing reasons. They'd tell you off for a cheeky remark but it wouldn't change their opinion of your skills on the pitch; they'd tell you off, move on and forget about it.

The same was not true of the next academy director, who took over at more or less the same time as I began my apprenticeship. This was when stuff started to get hard for me in football. Up until then, I had led a bit of a charmed footballing life, you might say. It was a simple process that began with me getting on the team, then getting the, ball, then scoring the goals that kept me on the team. Upfront, you have one job and that is to score goals. If you're scoring goals, you're doing your job, and if you're doing your job, you stay on the team.

Right?

Well, not always. I never had a problem with any of my managers or coaches but this guy had a problem with me. He used to play me (because: goals) but any opportunity to deny me a leg-up, he'd take it. If there was a chance for a player to go and train with the first team, he'd put anyone else up for it apart from me, even though I might have scored a hat-trick at the weekend. If I was requested, then of course I had to go. But if he could keep me back then he'd do it.

Thing is, with me, it's the bitchiness I can't handle. I don't mind someone telling me something to my face. I can take that all day. I'll handle it and won't hold a grudge. What I don't like is somebody who smiles to your face and then shits on you behind your back, and that's what he was like. Steve and Brian, they'd tell you something to your face. Not this one.

Fortunately, I benefited from the fact that the first-team manager, Iain Dowie, would often come and watch us play. Iain was an absolute legend. He knew everyone's name at the academy, which is pretty much unheard of for a first-team manager, and what's more, he had his eye on me. It was he who decided that I should start training and playing reserve games with the first team.

That preseason, I played every single minute of every single pre-season game. Next thing you know, I was on the bench for the first-team games – and desperate to show the world what I was capable of.

CHAPTER 11

Because I was a local lad and had played in the reserves, as well as being a bit of a pre-season star, I'd already built up a name among the fans. At half-time I'd always do tricks. I used to go and chat to fans, too, so there was a bit of recognition there.

I mention that as background to this part of the tale, which takes place ten games before the end of the 2007/08 season, when I was on the bench for a home game, just sitting there thinking, *Oh my God, this is it. I'm sitting on the bench, waiting for a game. This is it, man. This is it.* Then I heard my name being called out.

Ashley Cain, Ashley Cain, Ashley Cain.

They were chanting it. The crowd were chanting my name, imploring the manager to bring me on.

I sat there going hot and cold, thoughts running riot at the sound of my own name being sung by the fans. It struck me that I had friends and family in the stadium. And how my grandad, who had done nothing but support and encourage me on my footballing journey, would be hearing the fans chanting my name, and, God, that felt good. That felt really good. It felt as though I was repaying him for all those cold nights on the touchline in far less glamorous surroundings. Uncomplaining, unstinting support.

Wouldn't it be great to say that the manager listened to the crowd and brought me on?

He didn't. I stayed on the bench.

Next, we travelled to Plymouth and I thought, *This is it, this is the big one. I'm going to get a game.* I mean, it wouldn't have been quite so sweet, making my debut at an away fixture, but it didn't happen anyway, so that was the end of that.

The next home game was us hosting Charlton. My grandad had placed a £10 accumulator on that I'd make my debut, score, we'd beat Charlton, and that Charlton would get relegated as a result. If the whole sequence of events had panned out the way he wanted he would win an enormous amount of money, I think in the region of eight grand.

So anyway, the game was on, we were nil-nil and the crowd started up, 'Ashley Cain, Ashley Cain, Ashley Cain.'

I steeled myself.

'Ash, get warm,' said the manager.

I hopped off the bench, began running up and down the touchline, hardly even allowing myself to believe that I might get a game.

'Ash, over here,' he said, and I jogged back to him.

'Go on, son, you're going on,' he said, and the next thing I knew I was on the pitch.

It's difficult to describe the feeling. My adrenaline was off the charts. I mean, I'd been playing football since I was five years old. I knew about the game. I knew about the pressure. I knew what was expected of me. But now, all of a sudden, I didn't. It was like everything was distorted. I distinctly remember praying that the ball wouldn't come near me because, for the first few minutes at least, I just needed time to settle in and get my bearings.

And then it did – the ball came to me, and I was running with it. Doing my thing, aiming direct at defenders. And I could hear the crowd going mad. It was just like the reserves, just like all the youth team games I played. Me getting the ball was lifting the crowd. It would come to me and there would be a surge of anticipation running around the ground. As a player, that really lights a fire in your belly. It's not like I ever needed any encouragement to go out there and win – like I say, that competitiveness was baked into my DNA, but having the crowd behind me like that, willing me to press forward and score, was something else I talked before, about how having supporters on the challenges really inspires me. It's a feeling I recognise from those days at Coventry and I still recognise it now. From those early experiences, being cheered on by a crowd, I now know the power of support when times are tough. When I need to dig deep to complete my challenges, sometimes having the crowd behind me will make all the difference to spur me on to reach my goals.

Next thing you know, I was on the halfway line, seeing that we were creeping forward, receiving the ball, and driving forward. There was one of their full-backs to defeat and I jinked easily past him, putting myself through on goal with just the keeper to beat.

What happened next was, well, you'd have to call it a learning experience. Something that I've never forgotten, something I've taken with me for the rest of my life.

First thing to say is that I used to have this strange way of striking a ball. I would come at the ball from the right, and because of that I would always hit it with the outside of my boot and bend it. It was an unorthodox way of kicking a ball. No coach in the world would teach a kid to kick a ball the way that I did. But that's how I did it. And I became a specialist at it. A succession of coaches and managers would say, 'Don't hit it like that, strike it properly.' But I used to score an insane amount of goals that way.

So anyway, I've knocked the ball past the last defender, and I'm one-on-one with the keeper, and this is the way my thoughts went.

I'm making made my debut. It's nil-nil. I'm going to score my first goal. I'm going to relegate Charlton. I'm going to make my grandad rich.

I was about to shoot – shoot the way I always did, with the outside of my boot – and at the same time the next thought that flashed across my mind was my manager telling me, 'Don't hit it like that, strike it properly.'

And I realised that if I hit the ball with the outside of my boot and missed, then I was going to get the bollocking of all time. And at the very last millisecond, I checked myself, changed my mind and struck it the normal way.

And because the normal way wasn't my natural way, I pulled it, and the ball hit the outside of the post and pinged off for a goal kick.

So the score remained at nil-nil. I didn't score that game. I didn't relegate Charlton. I didn't make my grandad rich.

And even now, I think my life would have been different if I'd scored that goal. I think that it would have changed how people saw me in the footballing world. The fact was that I had a lot of eyes on me at that time because I was so quick, and that goal would have proved that my game wasn't limited to speed. It was evident to all that I was dangerous, but it would have proved that I could be clinical as well. People would have seen me as a game-changer, the way they see Jack Grealish now. A kid who's come on for twenty minutes, changed the game, scored the winning goal. An impact player.

I don't look back at football now and think I wish I was still playing. Like I said earlier, it just wasn't a passion for me. I did it because I was good at it, not because I had a drive to do it. I recognise this part of me now and that drive I need to succeed, to be strong, to give hope to others. But I'd be lying if I said that I don't look back on missing that goal and think what might have been. It's not as though I regret it. 'Regret' is the wrong word because I try never to regret anything; I try to learn from it. I keep in mind that if I think or do something it was me and me alone who chose to do it. I did that thing the way I wanted to do it; I did it to the best of my ability. And if it went wrong and what I did was a mistake then I was the one who chose to make that mistake.

My mistake in that situation? Well, I didn't listen to myself. I listened to what other people had been telling me, and because I listened to my head and not my heart my whole future changed. Had I struck the ball the way I was most comfortable with, then who knows? It might have gone in. And if it had gone in, well, everybody's happy.

If I'd struck the ball in the way I was most comfortable and it had still missed, then at least I'd have only myself to blame. The choice would have been mine and mine alone, not me trying to carry out a decision made by somebody else.

It keeps me awake, it still does. For years afterwards I was all twisted up inside, riven with guilt for not doing what I really wanted. I got a bit stuck with it. I'd think, *I should have scored. I should have scored.* It's not like when Marcus Rashford steps up to take a penalty he only has the keeper to beat, he also has all that pressure on his shoulders. Me, I had no pressure. I was just a young kid coming on for his debut. All the factors were in my favour. I should have scored.

CHAPTER 12

There were three games before the end of the season. One was away at Ipswich, who at that time were managed by Man United legend and a huge hero of mine, Roy Keane. I still remember being like *Roy Keane! I'm playing Roy Keane's team against Giovani dos Santos!*

It was a pretty good game. Not my best, but still pretty good. And then that was it. End of season. I played those last three games and it was pretty cool. After that came the issue of whether I'd be awarded a full-time professional contract.

It was funny because every contract I'd had up until then, literally from the age of ten, I kind of knew I was getting it. This was the first time that I really had no idea whether or not I was going to continue on my footballing journey. Along with my mum and dad I went along to the training ground, and I thought, *Well, maybe they're going to let me go, Mum and Dad are here to help pick up the pieces.* After all, I'd seen it happen to other kids. Kids whose only thought since they could kick a ball was to be a professional football player, their dreams in ruins. I'd heard the cries of anguish and seen the tears. How people can do that to kids, I really don't know, but it happens. It happens at every club every year. Kids' dreams die.

But not to me. Not that time. Mum and Dad were there to witness the fact that I was given a one-year pro contract for the first team with Coventry.

I think I was one of only four who got a contract that year. Eighteen were let go. My brother, Matty, who'd been with the academy at Leicester, got released at fifteen, and my dad had been through all that with him.

Once again, I played every single minute of every pre-season game. I scored a few, but I was more about creating chances. I'd frighten the defence; I'd send balls across the goal-face, win free kicks and create chances. I was doing so well that I was pretty much the out-and-out pick for this position, feeling on top of the world, like I was going to play all next season's games.

I look back on that time as being one of the best periods of my life. In fact, I'd go as far as saying that before Azaylia, the ages of seventeen to eighteen were my favourite because it was a time when I thought I was a man but had none of the responsibilities of being one. A time when it felt as though the world of football and therefore the world at large was my oyster. Even back then I wasn't big-headed enough to think that I could do literally anything. But then again, maybe I was, because it felt like I could.

And then guess what? The fucking gaffer only goes and buys a new winger.

CHAPTER 13

You don't get warned. You certainly don't get a reason why – other than the gaffer wants options upfront. All that happens is that one day you're the preferred winger, the next day a new arrival has his own seat in the dressing room. Not only that, but there was another midfielder arriving on loan. You might have heard of him, he's the current Liverpool and England midfielder: Jordan Henderson.

During the pre-season we'd played Everton, and after that, my agent got word that they'd been impressed with me. Everton are a Premiership side, of course. Coventry City were a Championship side. So a good step up if I could make it, and I was touted as a pretty big prospect at that time, so it felt achievable.

But Everton, if they wanted to sign me, needed to see me play. I mean, if you want to buy a car you might go to the showroom and see a car that takes your fancy, but you're not going to buy it without a test drive, are you? There are certain checks you need to make. For that reason I was desperate to get on and show what I could do. I wanted to score goals for Coventry and repay the fans' faith in me. I wanted to impress Everton. I wanted to prove that all this buzz around me wasn't just empty hype but fully justified. I wanted to show the world that I was the man.

But I couldn't get a game. The gaffer put me on the bench. I had to sit and watch other players doing the business – the business that I should have been doing.

Aagh, man, it was gutting. I think I got to play five games that season. *The whole season.*

This is when it starts to get difficult in football. It's certainly when it started to get difficult for me. I couldn't understand how I could do so well in pre-season, be the fittest, the quickest, the strongest, be scoring goals and performing well and then …

Spend the whole season on the bench. I just wasn't in the mix any more.

The next year or so I was in a state of flux. I went to Luton on loan but it wasn't a good fit for me for many reasons. So I went back to Coventry. Then Oxford were interested in me, so I went there on loan, played two games, came back.

Next stop was Port Vale, again on loan. There I got a game, went in for a tackle and …

Bang.

The guy went through me. By which I mean he smashed right into me, studs up, and in response my foot swivelled around as though it had decided to face the other way for a change.

Result? Broken ankle. I was out in need of surgery, and when I say out, I mean out – out-out. I would be laid up for three or four months.

But even then, I thought I'd be okay. The manager, Chris Coleman, liked me. After all, he had given me my pro contract, he'd played me at least eight times; I'd been a good lad and gained a bit of experience by joining other sides on loan. Sure, I was injured, but I'd be all right. That's the absolute truth in football: as long as the gaffer likes you, you'll be okay just as long as they don't get sacked.

You know what I'm going to say here, don't you?

That's right. He got sacked.

The new manager came in: Aidy Boothroyd. No doubt he took one look at my name on a list, thought, *I don't really know this kid and he's going to be out for three months, so there's no point in giving him a contract.*

So I was out.

And the maddest thing was that the next season, Coventry went into administration and lost pretty much all of its first team, as a result of which, first-year pros and some YTS players were playing. In other words, if I'd stayed, I would have played. I would have been a senior, experienced member of the squad, and I would have played all fucking season.

Gutted. Absolutely gutted.

CHAPTER 14

You know what? It's hard to tell this story – my story and
that of Azaylia – without it seeming like there's an awful
lot of bad luck involved. In athletics, I tore through my groin
in the final of the Triple-A's, which would have qualified me
for the internationals if I'd got through. In football, I ended up
losing a testicle, broke my ankle and … Well, believe me when I
say there's a lot more to come. I'm the guy who forgets to insure
his car and gets it stolen. And then, of course, the big one.

But what I've tried to do throughout my life, even – and
probably especially – during those times when I was on the
cusp of big things only to have bad luck strike, is stay positive.
What I did and still do to counter the dark thoughts is to sit
and think, okay, God blessed me with athletic ability. He
made me fast, aggressive and tenacious; he's made me not give
a fuck what anyone says about me, which has paid dividends
across all aspects of my life. He's given me a good brain and a

good and pure heart. And I need all of those things in order to raise money, raise awareness and honour Azaylia. And the bad luck that I've had in life has only made me stronger. It's only increased the quality of those assets.

But, yeah, no doubt about it, I've had some bad luck.

For example, still recovering from my ankle injury I was offered a place on an Olympic trial programme. It was a mixture of powerlifting, bobsleighing, velodrome cycling, and it would have been great, but of course I couldn't do it because my ankle was still an issue. So I missed out.

Out of contract. Out of work. Can't even do any pre-season trials because of my injury. And now that.

I was down, low, stressed, watching players that I knew get on with their careers and do well with their clubs, feeling like I was at a party but nobody would ask me to dance. The days of having a 10-foot picture of myself at the Ricoh Arena in Coventry were in the recent past but already felt like a distant memory. I'm not one to feel sorry for myself, I'm really not (see above for details), but I've got to say that I was pretty down back then. Things just looked ... bleak.

In the end, it was Mansfield Town who took a punt on me. I mean, look, Mansfield Town were not the heady heights of Coventry or Everton. A Conference side, they were not as high up in English football as I felt I should have been, but they had something that no other English club had at the time: they had faith in me.

So that's where I found myself for the 2010/11 season. Obviously, I couldn't start the season because I was injured, but I had a team at least, and what's more, they paid well and were a really good group of lads.

I turned up there, my normal loud and confident self, and although the manager thought I was a bit of a big-time Charlie, I soon became quite influential in the dressing room. Around that time I had a lot of what you might call 'side hustles' going on – we won't go into specifics, let's just leave it at that – and obviously there were other players who wanted in on the action.

So that was good. After such an unsettling period, I felt as though I was finding my feet again. Any problems? Of course there were.

The manager wouldn't play me. Fair enough, at first. After all, I was still recovering from my ankle operation. But when I started to train and my fitness returned, he still didn't put me in the team.

And then he still didn't put me in, and he still didn't put me in, and I was thinking to myself, *What the hell am I doing here? I'm fit, I'm healthy, but I'm not playing.*

I've always known that the game of football was unfair, but at this point I gained the maturity to understand that I couldn't worry about all the things that I couldn't control. It was down to me to focus on being the best player – it didn't matter what was going on around me in this game, the opinions, the decisions, the unfairness. It was about me now. It was always about me and making sure that, regardless of what was happening, I was ready for when my opportunity came. And this is what I'm saying. This is what I'm trying to tell you about football. This guy was our manager, but we had an assistant manager, Duncan Russell, who liked me. When the manager got sacked and Russ became manager, I played every single game. Right from his very first game in charge, I was in the side. I didn't do anything different. I didn't change my playing style, my attitude, nothing. It was just a question of personalities. The manager thought I was too big for my boots and needed taking down a peg, the assistant manager made a more sound footballing decision. And I'm not just saying that – that first game, when he put me in? I got three assists.

To be honest, it's been a big problem throughout my life. I can and do get on with anybody. Doesn't matter the age, gender, race, religion or background, everyone's the same to me. I'll get on with anyone just the same. Where I struggle is with authority. And it's not just that I struggle with authority, it's that authority struggles with me. I think it's my confidence that rubs people up the wrong way. And the fact that if you try to control me, I'll react against it. That new gaffer who came in was a Jack-the-lad. I could banter him, he could banter me. There was no competition between us.

And he kept playing me. I played and played until I got my big chance when we reached the FA Trophy semi-final. This was a game that if we won it, we would go on to play at Wembley.

At the same time, Derby County had shown an interest in me and wanted me to go and train with them. My gaffer – who liked me, remember – saw no problem in me going along. His only stipulation was that he wanted me for this semi-final. In terms of the league our season was more or less over, but we had a real chance of making it to the final of the FA Trophy. And I was a key team member then. I'd only scored two goals but my assist ratio was ridiculous; I had about twenty-five. And for that reason the strikers wanted me on the pitch. They knew I was going to get the ball into the box.

So we went to this semi-final against Luton, who were top of the league at the time. I knew the team well, of course, having been on loan there, so I was well aware that theirs is a daunting ground.

The match was to be played over two legs and we hosted them at home first. I was really getting into the game, thinking that this was my big chance to play at Wembley.

The second leg came around and I can't remember whether we were chasing the game or trying to break the deadlock. I don't suppose it really matters. What matters is that one of their players came in for a challenge and ...

Bang.

The next thing you know, I was in excruciating pain. It was as though somebody had taken a hammer and chisel to my upper leg.

Down I went, writhing on the floor in agony, clutching my thigh, which was filling up with blood – I could literally see it expanding before my eyes – thinking, *I'm fucked, I'm fucked, I'm fucked.* Testicle. Ankle. And now my fucking leg.

As they stretchered me off, my hands were at my face, and within the pain was the one thought: Derby. My chances of being signed by them, of getting back into the Championship were gone. With one reckless tackle, they had been shattered.

After going to the medical centre to get it bandaged to keep it compressed, I was supplied with crutches and allowed to rejoin my team, who were celebrating an historic win over Luton, one that had put us into the final at Wembley. There was still a bit of time before the final, and I hadn't yet been fully diagnosed, so there was a little, actually quite large and hopeful, part of me thinking that maybe I could still play a part.

It now looks like hopeless naïveté, of course. But that's because I didn't know then what I know now: I had a complete rupture in my quadricep.

Anyway, I was drinking, celebrating, not really thinking about it, until a day later I got a call from the gaffer: 'How are you, mate?'

'Well, I'm not okay, I'll come in tomorrow and go to the physio.'

So I went in. Now, the difference between a big club like Coventry and a club like Mansfield is that at Coventry, if anything happens, you go for a scan that day. At Coventry, I was in that scanning machine more times than I can count. Even if it was just a tear or pull, I'd go to get a scan. Cost: £2,000 a time.

But now I was with Mansfield, and they don't send you for a scan. They can't afford it. Instead there was this physio giving me deep-tissue massage. Now, I'd completely ruptured my quad. Didn't know it at the time, but that was the problem, because you do not initially treat a ruptured quadricep with deep-tissue massage. It doesn't help the injury and it's very, very painful.

I was screaming in agony – so loudly that the director's wife came down to ask what was going on. The physio was like, 'No, he needs it, he needs it.' And so I gritted my teeth and submitted to the pain, thinking that whatever he did, it had to help. The gaffer wanted me to play, but more to the point, I wanted to play, because I still wanted to impress Derby. Whatever happened, I had to play in the final against Darlington.

CHAPTER 15

Leading up to the big day, I played five games and was in absolute agony for every one of them, running around with stiff legs, gritting my teeth against the extreme pain. Still, I was determined not to blow this chance.

So it got to the final: 7 May 2011. I could hardly move, but I wanted to play. I thought, if I can play five games running around in pain then I can play this one at Wembley. At least I can grace the hallowed turf. Days before the game I'd been on my hands and knees feeling the pitch, picking up a bit of turf, putting it in my pocket, eating a bit of grass, lying on it like a starfish. The pitch was like a carpet.

There were 40,000 people in. My family were in the stands, too. I sat on the bench waiting for my chance. The game was nil-nil. At ninety-five minutes, during extra time, I came on.

We piled on the pressure. Playing through the pain, I crossed one over, but Paul Connor headed it over the bar, which was perhaps our best chance of that period.

And then, four minutes before the end of extra time, just as it looked like the final would go to penalties, Chris Senior scored for Darlington, and that was it. The dream was over.

Personally I had put everything I had into it, and as I limped off, I knew full well that there was going to be no football in my immediate future. My own bitter diagnosis was that I'd need three months to get fit.

And in the off-season you get six weeks.

There were words between me and the chairman. I went on holiday to Marbella, during which time I got a call from the club, telling me that I wasn't coming back. Derby had lost interest, too. Instead I ended up signing for another Conference side, Tamworth, although once again, my injury meant I couldn't start at the beginning of the season and, on top of that, those problems I'd had with my managers reared their head again – you know by now I'm a strong character and he clearly felt threatened by my sway in the changing room – so I was quickly sent to Telford, again in the Conference. By now, I was beginning to see a pattern: injury, problem with the manager, injury, problem with the manager, repeat till fade. And I was still only in the Conference, still a long way from where I wanted to be, which was the Championship and, ideally, the Premiership.

I was losing my love for the game.

But, you know, what can you do? I bit the bullet, gritted my teeth, and got on with the job at hand, which meant grinding out the rest of the season with Telford then returning to Tamworth.

I could have stayed at Tamworth if I wanted, but although I liked it there, and I really enjoyed the dressing-room culture, it still was nowhere near where I wanted to be. So when I got a new agent, who fixed me up with an opportunity in Romania, a club called CS Gaz Metan Mediaș, I didn't need to think about it about it for too long.

You don't sign straight away, of course. You need to show them you can do the business and so I flew over there, only to be greeted by a sweltering hot Romanian summer. I had a first training session and went into a trial game. I did well. I scored a hat-trick. So that was enough for them. I played my first proper game, scored two goals, then went on to play my second game and scored another hat-trick.

All of a sudden, they were waving the promise of a four-year contract under my nose. This was the first time since becoming a pro I'd been offered that kind of security. Not only that, but they started off offering me 10 grand a month, then 15, then upgraded it to 20 grand a month, with a pay increase every year, plus bonuses. I was like, *Yes, bring it on.*

CHAPTER 16

Romania was mad. Back then I was as big as I am now – I'd been training like an absolute beast – I had loads of tats and at that time was sporting a Mohican with tramlines down the side.

I'm telling you, in Romania this made me some kind of exotic species. People would literally come up to me in the street, just to touch me. I was treated like some kind of celebrity.

'I will look after you now,' I was told on one occasion, called over to some guy's table in a nightclub. I loved it. I thought, *Yeah, I could really get on here.*

Pre-season with CSG continued at the same time as my contract negotiations. The team flew to Budapest in Hungary for the last game of the tour, and it was while we were out there preparing for the match that my agent got in touch to say that the bartering was finally complete. After the game, I'd fly back to Romania, sign on the dotted line and spend the next four years being a very well-paid player in Liga I of the Romanian football league.

Finally – *finally* – things were working out. They were going my way.

As I went onto the pitch at the beginning of the match, a translator came running over to me, telling me that they wanted me on the other side for kick-off. *Fine*, I thought, *doesn't matter much to me*. During that period, I was playing for fun, just enjoying my football again, plus I was thinking that the next day I'd be returning to sign a contract that would bring me at least 20 grand a month for the next four years. That's like over three million.

I'm going to be a millionaire, I was thinking. *I'm going to be a millionaire.*

The whistle blew. The ball came my way, I jumped to flick it on, landed and …

Bang.

I hit the deck. Behind me I could see a player, and it was him who I assumed had clattered into me, sending me to the ground.

I was screaming, 'Get him off. Fucking send him off,' before becoming aware that other players were gesticulating. 'No, no one near you,' they were saying, 'No one near you.' They looked shocked, some of them ashen-faced. Gazing around the stadium, I could see fans with their hands clutching their heads or clasped over their mouths. I glanced over to the bench, where everybody had stood up.

What was wrong with that lot? Why was the physio grabbing his bag and adopting that quick, hunched-over run in order to tear across the turf and reach me as quickly as possible?

I tried to pull myself off the grass but it was immediately apparent that something wasn't right. I can only describe it as a flopping. Instead of responding to my desire to stand, the leg just ... flopped.

The physio skidded to a halt beside me, dropped to his knees and his hands went to my ankle. Almost the moment they did, he looked up at me. I looked up at him.

'I've snapped it, haven't I?' I said to him.

We both knew what I meant. My Achilles had gone. It wasn't sore like you get with Achilles tendinitis, it had completely ruptured and rolled right up into my calf.

The other thing that the physio and I both knew was that while it's not impossible to come back from that kind of injury, it's very, very difficult. In most cases it's a career-ending injury.

I learned later that they had heard the snap of it on the other side of the stadium.

Bandaged up and on the coach, I was in a state of shock. By then I had a good rapport with the other lads on the team, but as they gathered round to offer words of support and encouragement, trying to reassure me, I could sense their words were hollow. I was fucked.

I phoned my dad, who had been waiting to hear the news that I'd signed a new contract, not the news that I brought him.

'Dad, I've snapped my Achilles.'

To which his reply was, 'Oh, fuck.'

Then 'No ...' was all he could say and I could feel the devastation on the other end of the line.

They ended up getting me a taxi from Hungary to Romania so I could get my stuff, get to the airport, be wheeled through the terminal in a wheelchair and get on a flight to England and home.

The next day I was in London, where the best Achilles surgeon in the world, Professor Nicola Maffulli, took a look at me. According to him, the Achilles is so thick and strong that the conditions must have been perfect for it to snap. I must have landed in just the right – or wrong – way. The angle, the speed, the way I landed must all have been working against me in order to completely rupture it.

He's got its own method, this guy, the Maffulli technique. There were people from Barcelona, as in the club, watching because everything he does has such huge implications for the world of football.

But for me?

Nah. I was too far gone. I would have been better off snapping my leg in half than rupturing my Achilles. It just doesn't repair in the way torn muscles or broken bones do. So it didn't matter that I had the Maffulli technique. It didn't matter that I had the same never-say-die, can-do attitude that I do today. The injury was enough to stop me playing football and that's not because you can't walk or can't play the game. You can. It's because you'll never be the same player that you were. Like, when I run now, I'm not running the way I used to. In professional and elite sports you're talking about seconds, milliseconds, all of which make the difference. And the thing was that my game was all about pace. That's what made me stand out. Every single injury I had took a yard off my sharpness, a yard off my speed, and the Achilles injury was just the nail in the coffin. I can't push off it. I can't jump off it. I mean, I have played since, but at an even lower level. And it was never the same.

Not only that, but even if the operation is such a success that you come back as good as you were (which never happens), you're not talking four or five months' recovery time, you're talking twelve months.

So obviously, the contract never happened.

In fact, nothing happened.

And for the time being, my relationship with football just ground to a halt. You could be going out with the love of your life, but if they keep cheating on you, then one day you're going to fall out of love with them, and that's what happened to me with football. I felt like every opportunity I had, football cheated me. It cheated me and cheated me and cheated me. And in the end I just didn't want it any more. I didn't want to be fighting my way back from injury only to get another one. I didn't want to be sitting on my sofa for months every year, depressed because of the opportunities I was missing. Depressed that I was missing out because the gaffer didn't like me as a person. Depressed thinking about what I could have been.

It was hard, I can't tell a lie, and it certainly didn't happen overnight, but in the end I had no other choice but to move on. The question was, what to do next?

Part Three

THE WORLD OF REALITY TV

CHAPTER 17

Picture the scene. It's June 2012, I'm twenty-one years old, and instead of enjoying my youth and the fruits of my footballing labour, barrelling around in an Audi with Louboutin bags in the back, I'm lying on a sofa in my rented flat, wondering where the next penny is going to come from.

Professor Maffulli had done an excellent repair job on my leg, but I was still out of action for the foreseeable. Unable to walk, unable to stand for long periods without crutches, and needing to keep my foot raised in order to aid recovery, football was out of the question, and so was any other work. CSG had cut me loose, of course they had. I was no good to them. But being out of contract meant I had no insurance, and because the accident had happened outside the jurisdiction of the FA, it was also outside their remit, so they didn't come with any help for me, either.

I don't know if I was clinically depressed then. It certainly felt like it. Ahead of me stretched twelve months of hardship, of being alone with my thoughts and having to contemplate the fact that my once-glittering career was a nonstarter. All that promise. Now, nothing.

Nowadays, I know that everything in life is preparation, which means that I can look back knowing that period was no different. From it I gained strength and I gained resilience. I developed mental muscles that would end up helping me with many of the trials to come. (Had I but known that this period would seem like a walk in the park compared to what fate had in store for me.) But at the time?

Hard. It was hard.

For a while I lasted on what meagre savings I had (and I've never been very good with money, so they were indeed meagre) and then after a few months, I was able to drive again, provided it was an automatic. Then of course petrol was an issue, as in, affording the fuel, and I remember scrounging down the cushions of the sofa for loose change in order to put fuel in the car. Emptying out pots of shrapnel.

And it's funny, because in a sense my newfound relative hardship actually helped the injury heal. It meant that I had no choice but to walk, whether I liked it or not. Walking became an enforced part of my rehab and I believe that mobility was what helped me get back on my feet earlier than I otherwise might have done.

I graduated from walking to cycling everywhere. I'd bike to the gym, do my session then ride back. If I wanted to go see my nan or my mum, I'd either cycle or run round to their houses.

So, I got my mobility back, and as I moved on from the rehab stage of my recovery, I began training and getting pretty fit.

I wasn't even sure what my endgame was. Just that there was no point in lying around on the sofa feeling sorry for myself. Thing is, that just isn't me. I'm like the great white shark that dies if it stops moving. So I'm feeling better physically, and you better know that with fitness comes an improved state of mind. I tore up my invite to the pity party. So now the main problem was that I still didn't have any cash. My friends would be, 'Yo, come out tonight, Ash,' and I'd be having to plead poverty.

Until, one night, my mate got fed up with me knocking him back and offered to pay, and so we went out together. I can't remember where exactly, just some club. The point being that inside I saw a guy who was using the very first e-cigarette I'd ever seen.

These days we know them as vapes, of course. But back then, they were e-cigarettes, and they were styled to look just like normal cigarettes. This was some five years after the smoking ban; you weren't allowed to smoke a proper fag inside a pub or nightclub. But an e-cigarette? That was fine.

Not only did this guy get to 'smoke' inside, but I couldn't help but notice that he was also getting a huge amount of attention. It was like a showpiece, everyone was drawn to it. It might sound stupid – nowadays, everyone's smoking vape pens, nobody bats an eyelid – but back then, it was a novelty.

That night I lay in bed, a bit drunk, thinking of all the attention he was getting. One thing I knew was that in club world, attention is all. Attention is currency. Back in the days when I'd had money, we used to get a table in a nightclub. And at that table we'd order hundreds of pounds' worth of drink, because if you've got bottles on the table, then that's where the attention is, and that's where the girls go.

Attention. Girls. That's it. If you can crack that in the nightclub world then you've cracked that world.

The next day, I started looking into e-cigarettes. Back then, they were mainly seen as an alternative to cigarettes for those trying to give up, the idea being that you'd ditch normal fags, go to the e-cigarette variety, and gradually wean yourself off altogether. Anybody using an e-cigarette up till then would probably have been having little inconspicuous drags, feeling a bit embarrassed by it. That's why you never really saw them.

My guy in the club had flipped the script. He was drawing the e-cigarette out of the shadows and making it the hero of his story. That day I began to think about taking the idea a step on. If you're going to make a virtue of your e-cigarette, then make it look *cool*. Pimp it out. Bling it up. Own that shit.

One drawback was the nicotine. Thinking about my immediate network, I knew that if I created a standard e-cigarette brand then the footballers and athletes in my contacts book wouldn't be interested because they don't want nicotine, full stop. Matter of fact, there's a vast amount of non-athletic people who don't want to inhale an addictive and harmful substance. Cigarettes were no longer the thing. Just the pictures on a fag packet would turn your stomach. Nicotine, too, had fallen out of favour.

But alcohol? Everybody loved a booze. So the idea I came up with was for a brand of *nicotine-free* e-cigarettes, which would be flavoured like alcoholic drinks. I'd have rum and coke, strawberry daiquiri, raspberry vodka. Nothing intoxicating about them, just the taste of the drink. I decided to call it Hard Candy.

CHAPTER 18

So I had an idea. What I didn't have was business experience or acumen. Plus, of course, I had a forbiddingly empty bank account with no real prospects of it filling up any time soon.

Back to Google I went. There, I found a site called LinkedIn – again, it was still pretty new at the time – where I searched for users who were doing things in this field, found a guy in Leicester who was starting a business and looking for a partner, and emailed him.

I mentioned that I was an ex-professional football player and that I had excellent contacts in the world of football and also in the club world. I also mentioned that I had an idea that he'd be interested in. Did he want to meet? Yes, he did.

This guy turned out to be a slightly shy and retiring guy who was the complete opposite to me. He had some money behind him, and the fact that he'd entered the e-cigarette market early was commendable, but as it turned out, his product wasn't that great. I think he was aware of that, as a result of which he embraced my idea. He could see that what I envisioned was taking the whole e-cigarette thing to the next level.

In other words, our different skillsets complemented one another. In terms of a partnership, he brought the money and business experience, whereas I was able to add a fresh perspective, as well as providing the operation with a figurehead and plenty of contacts.

To cut a long story short, we went in with each other, refined the concept, designed the product, and placed an order for a sample of 100.

When they arrived, I dragged my partner out to a club, where I made sure I was seen with the first-ever Hard Candy e-cigarette. To say it went well is an understatement. By the end of the night we'd sold them all at a tenner each, including the one I'd been using for demonstration purposes.

Around this time, I was fiddling around on an iPad when something came through from the TV show *Take Me Out*. I'd been applying for all kinds of stuff. I mean, *all kinds*. Also, there had been a time, just before I went to Romania, when I'd gone to live in the *Big Brother* house as a kind of guinea pig. It was a cross between an audition, a screen test, and a technical rehearsal for the *Big Brother* people, but it never came to anything because I'd decided I wanted to go and play football in Romania instead.

Either way, it was no doubt doing that which had put me on the radar of whoever it was that emailed me about *Take Me Out*. That's the way it works. You apply, you get on the books. Other things crop up as a result.

Take Me Out, just in case you're not familiar with it, was a dating show on ITV. Hosted by Paddy McGuinness, the idea of it was that a single man (me, in this case) would try to impress thirty women who stood behind plinths on which there was a light. As the game progressed, they could turn off their light if they didn't want a date. If the game ended and no lights were on, that was called a blackout, and the guy would leave with his tail between his legs. If some lights were on, then it was up to the guy to choose his date.

I went down to London, did the audition, got chosen, returned home, borrowed some money off my Auntie Michelle because I couldn't afford any new gear to wear, then went and filmed the show.

It was brilliant. I really enjoyed it. Nobody turned their light off at the start, nor on the second round. It was funny because when I said I was a footballer, quite a few lights went out, which says a lot for the reputation of footballers. Even so, I got my date with a girl called Rach.

The date itself was okay. The thing with going on TV you soon discover is that some people are ready to give everything out whereas others are quite reserved. You won't be surprised to learn that I was in the former category. Rach was in the latter. We didn't quite gel in that respect and there was no real romantic spark.

The other issue with the date itself was the whole Fernando's experience. At *Take Me Out* they call the island Fernando's, but in fact it's a northern coast in Tenerife. It all sounds lovely, but the problem is that you fly out on the day, go on your date that night, and then the next day you're flying home. It's not like you ever get the chance to have fun and properly get to know each other; it's really more of a brief meet, most of which is dictated by the needs of the crew, who have to get material for broadcast.

There was a while to wait before the show was broadcast – it eventually went out in February 2013 – and so I cracked on with Hard Candy in the meantime. By now we were selling them everywhere we went, mainly nightclubs but also shops and other retailers, and we were doing really well with them. Next, my episode of *Take Me Out* was shown on TV.

These days, if you're a contestant on something like *Take Me Out*, it's really no big deal, but back then things were different. Reality TV was big, but there was nowhere near as much of it as there is now, so there wasn't a surplus of 'reality TV stars' clogging up the airwaves. What's more, this was a time before influencers. Like I say, I had stood out on the show.

As a result, I was suddenly a bit of a big noise, a minor TV star, just because of that one appearance on that one programme. I was getting asked to do personal appearances at clubs based on the fact that I'd been on TV, and of course every time I did an appearance I'd take my Hard Candy products with me in order to sell them (see? I told you I was a hustler).

At the club they'd sit me on some kind of VIP table. I'd be puffing away on my Hard Candy, and clubgoers would be interested, the manager would be shimmying over, saying, 'What's that? Let's have a look at that.'

I'd show him, and …

'We got to have those behind the bar.'

So now this club's got the product, and that club's got the product, and the next club's got the product. Until we got to the point where most of the big clubs in the UK had Hard Candy behind the bar.

Off the back of that, I launched the Hard Candy parties. I'd do nights where not only was I taking the door money, like a normal promoter would, but I was getting my product in the clubs and selling that, too. I'd have a stand in the club with girls flogging the product so that I'd be making, say, £4,000 on the door and then another £4,000 with the product inside. Birmingham on a Friday night, Manchester on a Saturday night. Things were going really well.

CHAPTER 19

I won't go into details, but matters began to get a bit strained between me and my Hard Candy partner. On a personal note, another issue was the business being mainly a night-time operation, which meant that I'd often spend days sitting on my arse not doing much. If you know anything about me by now, you know this isn't a good thing for me.

Right, I thought, *I need a job*, and so started applying. At the same time, I began playing part-time football for a non-league side, for which I got paid a couple of hundred quid a week. I'm not gonna lie, it wasn't the most challenging football I've played in my life. I mean, I was an ex-Championship player. I didn't go to training, I just turned up on a Saturday and played, and I tended to do really well.

As far as my love life was concerned, I was in this relationship with a girl, Talitha. It had been on the cards for a while that we needed to split up. It was as simple as that.

We really liked each other but were better apart than we were together.

So that's what was going on in my life at the time: building up Hard Candy, playing football at the weekend, navigating the turbulent waters of my love life. And to be honest, with the exception of the relationship, things were pretty rosy.

Until one night when the relationship situation was resolved: Talitha and I split up. Which, like I say, was the best thing for both of us. The next morning was a Sunday, and I was lying in bed alone, just hanging, when the phone went.

'Hey, this is Steve from MTV, how you doing?'

'Oh, do fuck off, mate,' I said, and ended the call, wondering which one of my mates was trying to prank me.

It rang again, and this time the guy was speaking really quickly. 'Hi, mate, don't put the phone down, I promise you this really is Steve from MTV.'

'All right,' I said. 'Send me an email so I can see.'

A moment later, it pinged in my inbox: *Steve from MTV*. Needless to say, I was happy to speak to him.

As we hopped on another call, he asked how I was and I told him fine, except that I'd split up with my girlfriend the night before. That particular bit of information seemed to land well with him, for reasons that I didn't interrogate him much about at the time. He told me that they were working on a new show. 'Imagine *Geordie Shore* but abroad,' he told me. 'It's called *Summer of Love*. What a great way to get over an ex, eh?'

So, I thought, a *dating thing, then*.

'Yes, okay,' I said, 'maybe.'

'And the thing is we've been reaching out to try and find contestants on the show and our guys keep going to clubs and asking club owners if they know anybody who'd be good, and your name keeps coming up. You did *Take Me Out*, right?'

Yes, I agreed, I'd done *Take Me Out*.

'So we got your number and I thought I'd make contact.'

'Okay, sweet, cool,' I said.

In pretty short order, I had an audition which I went along to and was, well, 'myself'. The same 'myself' I was whether I was in an audition or schmoozing Hard Candy or out with my mates: confident, quite brash, full of smiles, fun-loving, loves to get his shirt off.

Off the back of my audition, they wanted me for the show. *Summer of Love*, it was still called, or so they said. All I knew was the title and that it would involve going somewhere abroad. Somewhere sunny. All sounded good to me.

My ex, Talitha, and I were still on speaking terms at this time, although we had a slightly competitive one-upmanship dynamic going on. You know how it is with breakups. You love the other party to know how well you're doing without them. We were no different, and one day she told me that she'd been cast in a new MTV show.

What was it called?

Yup. *Summer of Love*.

So that was interesting. Assuming it was no coincidence that they'd asked both me *and* her, the show obviously had an angle I hadn't been told about. As to how they got her, I honestly don't know how the production team do this kind of stuff. Perhaps they join the dots through social media. Either way, I kept schtum that I was on the show, too, and secretly enjoyed how frustrated she was that I was so laidback about her bit of good fortune.

The next thing, I discovered that I was flying out to Marbella for the show. It transpired that I would be travelling out some days before her.

That was interesting, too. It got me thinking that maybe I was a main cast member and she wasn't.

Even knowing that, I was still in the dark about the whole thing. This was the beauty of the show. Well, the *first season* of the show. Nobody had a clue what was going on. Once the format was established, of course, that element of surprise was lost and you got contestants who not only knew the format, but were very savvy as to how the game is played, and it kind of lost its magic a bit.

Back then, though – and the reason that the show, which was of course retitled *Ex on the Beach*, was a record-breaking show for MTV – nobody knew that the format involved cast members' exes appearing in order to stir up trouble. All the shocks and surprises were real.

Or, should I say *most* of the shocks and surprises. Like I say, I had insider information ...

As we assembled in the villa in Marbella, ten guys and girls all in our early twenties, all pretty fit – in both senses of the word – we took some time to acclimatise to the whole set-up. The villa used what they call a fixed-rig camera set-up, outside and inside, so you're filmed twenty-four hours a day. However, when you go on excursions, or when you go on a date, they break out the camera crew as well. In fact, we soon worked out that the appearance of a camera crew meant that something exciting was about to happen.

Not that we needed much added excitement. The fact was, we were like over-sugared hyperactive kids the whole time, having an absolute whale of a time in the villa and fully expecting that when the show was broadcast we were going to be the next big thing, the next *Geordie Shore*. Indeed, we had Vicky Pattison from *Geordie Shore* in the villa, while another two *Geordie Shore* cast members, Ricci Guarnaccio, and Dan Conn, joined us later on, which in our eyes was proof enough that MTV had ultimate faith in the show.

As for the central concept of our exes turning up to surprise us, I had let on that I knew Talitha was flying out, and so it wasn't that big a surprise – perhaps not as big as the production team had hoped – when the blasts-from-the-past began appearing.

Looking back, I remember having a great time, but I also know that I lost the plot on occasion. This was where the image that I lived with for many years to come began to mould. The thing was that being on *Take Me Out* and spending a week as a guinea pig in the *Big Brother* house was one thing, but it hadn't prepared me for the experience of being filmed around the clock. I was raw, man, not sure how to play the camera, or should I say play *to* the camera. Not sure how to rise to the occasion. I'd get angry; there would be outbursts. Some of them were shown on the show, some of them weren't.

I was a different person back then. I didn't have the same maturity that I do now. I've always prided myself on being a person who never acts differently to how I feel. I'm heart on sleeve. I'm heart forward. What you see is what you get. That's just the way I am. But it didn't mean it was all plain sailing.

The production team worked that out quickly. No doubt in their minds I was just a rough little townie liable to firework off at the slightest hint of provocation, and for them that was catnip. These programmes literally thrive on conflict, and the production team knew that if they wanted things to kick off then all they needed to do was prod me, and the way they decided to do that was by manipulating other cast members to bait me a bit.

I won't go into the nitty-gritty of it, not about this or any other show I've been on. This is because I don't want any 'sensational' or newsworthy aspects of my reality-TV life to overshadow what this book is really about. This is not a book about bickering kids in swimwear. It's about Azaylia.

Then again, you probably wouldn't be reading this if not for shows like *Ex on the Beach*, and for me, that experience was reality TV in a nutshell. You think it's all about going on there and acting natural, but in fact the producers are pushing and influencing certain situations, and they do that by having little private chats with certain cast members behind the scenes, asking him (or her) to go and do this, go and do that. They tried it with me a couple of times, but I was like, 'No, it's not what I want to do. I'm not an actor. I'm here because it's a reality TV show, I'm going to be myself.'

But there will always be others who are going to do as they're asked. Not because they're especially weak-minded or pliable but just because they want to get on and do well, or they think that by following orders they'll get more screen time. Or simply because they're asked to do something by the production team and so they do it, because the production team are the guys in charge.

Who knows? The point is that the one thing you can say about reality TV is that you can't trust anyone. The second you start believing people for whatever reason is when you're dead in the water. You watch these shows and you see contestants endlessly chewing over who's being 'fake' and who's being 'real'. I wouldn't go as far as saying that everybody is being fake, because I certainly wouldn't say that I was fake as such. But neither was I real. I was an exaggerated, heightened version of myself, and as far as I'm concerned, that's the same for everybody in there.

And actually, even though this is where my 'bad boy' legend got minted, I was far from the only one going nuts. No doubt about it, the shit got a bit crazy in there at times. None of us could really believe what was happening. Things weren't as politically correct back then as they are now, so we were that bit wilder than we would be if the show were broadcast these days (in fact, *Ex on the Beach* was cancelled in 2019 when they pulled the plug on the tenth season because one of the cast members had committed suicide between filming and broadcast). So it was basically the maddest, craziest holiday of your life, except turned up to ten because everybody was trying to perform, and I was no different.

CHAPTER 20

Talitha came on the show in the second week. It was probably by then that I had already established myself as a bit of a firebrand and things spiralled after that. Not deliberately; it just happened, for the reasons I said in the last chapter.

I hold my hands up. It wasn't great. It wasn't a good look for anybody, especially not for somebody whose every action is being broadcast on MTV. In the end, the producers just said, 'You've got to go. You're out of here.'

Even at the time I thought it was unfair. What did they expect to happen? After all, if you put a lion in a cage and keep on poking it, one day it's going to turn around and bite you. You might just lose a finger, but on the other hand it might take off your arm. If you don't want to lose your arm then you're best advised not to poke the thing in the first place.

They clearly knew *something* would happen. They certainly

had security on the scene quick enough. Either way, that was enough to get me the image of the bad boy of MTV.

Pretty different to the way I am now, right? But life is all about growth. I know that now. I know that better than anyone.

So, I got turfed off *Ex on the Beach* with my tail between my legs (yeah, right) one episode before the end, and I returned home from Marbella knowing that I'd have to wait six months for the show to be broadcast. I was pretty sure it was going to be a big show, and I also knew that I had the potential to be one of the standout cast members, so I was reasonably confident that good things were coming for me.

That still left me with six months to fill. And I filled it in by playing football, as well as getting a job as a sales rep at the David Lloyd leisure centre in Narborough. Basically, if somebody wanted to open a membership, I was the person they'd speak to.

At the same time, I was of course carrying on with the Hard Candy stuff. The days of getting PAs off the back of my appearance on *Take Me Out* were long gone, that particular fifteen minutes of fame having faded, but I was still doing the nights, still going to clubs and festivals selling the product, and the commercial/selling side of things was going really well.

As for the partnership side of things? That wasn't so great. I'm not gonna go into details here. Firstly, it would bore the pants off you. Secondly, there are probably legal ramifications, and thirdly, it's really not relevant to the story. But imagine somebody riding a bike with a wobbly wheel. It's getting wobblier and wobblier. At some point, it comes off.

But not just yet. I was still taking stands and salespeople

into venues, hustling and bustling, making a bit of money as I waited for *Ex on the Beach* to appear. At David Lloyd I was doing well, meeting my sales targets, and helping the club reach its overall targets.

Still, it was a bit like being back at school, in more ways than one. I'd be hitting my targets and doing well, but at the same time I'd be Jack-the-lad around the club and, as usual, I got off on the wrong foot with one of the managers. Same old story. And in the end, wouldn't you know it? I got the sack.

But, it didn't really matter. Why? *Ex on the Beach* was out. Life was about to change.

CHAPTER 21

So, I said that after doing *Take Me Out* I got offered PAs at nightclubs, which I did, and was very pleased to do them, too. A PA – personal appearance – involves literally getting paid just for turning up at a nightclub and being treated like a VIP guest, all on somebody else's tab. For a kid of twenty-two, which I was at the time, it was pretty much a dream gig.

But that was just me turning up by myself: Ashley Cain, him out of *Take Me Out*. When *Ex on the Beach* was broadcast the PA offers started rolling in again, except this was way different to before. Now, there was a lot more money involved, and they wanted more cast members. Plus, there was much more interest, hence more opportunities to do it.

What would happen was that they'd get four lads from *Ex on the Beach*: me, Marco (he was my boy), Jack and Liam, and we'd meet up in, say, Manchester, and do the whole weekend together. And 'doing the weekend' entailed literally nothing more than going along to a club, travel and hotel all paid for. It's not like we had to stand on stage and talk, or judge dancing competitions or anything like that. It was no more taxing than sitting in a VIP booth, drinking and having our picture taken.

I was still playing semi-pro football at the time, so I'd do gigs on Wednesday, Thursday, Friday nights, not really sleep, drive back home on Saturday morning, play football, go home, recover, get in the gym the next day and get back in shape for the next weekend – a weekend that, like I say, started on Wednesday.

That's it. It was unreal.

I mean, the reality TV bubble was just about at its peak back then. As reality TV stars, there were enough of us to make things interesting, but not so many that we were over-exposed. Boredom hadn't yet set in. We would go to a club, and it would be full of people there to see us. The DJs must have absolutely hated it. For that one night, nobody was looking at them, they were all looking at us.

And of course that meant a lot of girls. I wouldn't take one back to my hotel, I'd take a whole group. I'm not boasting, that's just the way it was. And the thing was that you could get away with it, it was almost expected of us.

It's not like I was wet behind the ears. I knew this kind of thing went on, but still, to actually *be the* guy was a different matter altogether. Looking back from where I am now, which is a very, very different place, I'm almost embarrassed to admit it, but at that point I thought, *I've made it. I've absolutely made it.* Every now and then MTV would call and I'd have to film, like, a trailer or something or do some bit of promotion for the show, which only added to my overall feeling of being Billy Big Bollocks.

But – and here's a big but – MTV had told us that *Ex on the Beach* was not to be a show like *The Only Way is Essex* or *Geordie Shore*. In other words, each series would have a different cast. We didn't find that out until after the show was over. During filming we were speaking to the producer, saying, 'Should we change our names? Should I be Ashley *Ex on the Beach*, like they do with *The Only Way is Essex* and *Geordie Shore*?'

But of course they were like, 'No, no, no, it's just not like that.'

I remember being pretty disappointed when I found that out. I knew from my experience with *Take Me Out* that the fame side of things comes quickly but goes just as quickly.

The upshot was that while we were all loving our time in the spotlight, for me it was slightly overshadowed by the knowledge that it was to be oh-so temporary. *Ex on the Beach* had been successful enough to guarantee a second season, but a second season meant a new bunch of cast members. Fresh meat. We would be yesterday's news. Last season. Nobody wants a PA from last season's *Ex on the Beach* star. Nobody wants last season's *Ex on the Beach* star drinking their vodka.

So I was living with that knowledge. Thinking, fine, just make hay while the sunshine is full, make the most of it, enjoy my time on the gravy train. After all, why not?

But then I got a call.

CHAPTER 22

MTV liked me. They were saying things like, 'You're explosive. You're great TV. We want you back.'

Back?

Yes. They wanted me to return for the second season. Just as I had been in football, a sub that could come on and potentially change the game, so it seems I would be with *Ex on the Beach*. Inviting me back for a return appearance, it was clear that MTV saw me as an impact player, someone who could come on, shake things up and make shit happen.

You can see exactly why they did it. What they didn't want was a whole bunch of new contestants who, having watched season one, thought they knew exactly how the game worked. They didn't want complacency. They wanted things shaken up.

And of course, shaking things up was well within my skill set. Always was, and I like to think still is. Being well-behaved?

Well, that's something that I've always struggled with, which is probably why the restrictions were in place.

Restrictions? Oh yes. There were a number of them. MTV didn't want me staying in the villa with the rest of the cast. Nor did they want me drinking. Nor did they want me getting off with any of the girls on the show. At a certain time of night I'd have to leave the villa and go back to my secret lair.

The second season of *Ex on the Beach* featured Charlotte Crosby and Gaz Beadle from *Geordie Shore*, as well as Jess Impiazzi, who had appeared on *The Only Way is Essex*. I sat most of it out, held back until episode seven, when I made my grand appearance to gasps from the assembled cast, who all knew who I was.

My ex was Emily Colley, and when my first job was to pick two girls to take to the penthouse for a jacuzzi party, I picked her, as well as a girl called Anita, who had been going out with Gaz from *Geordie Shore* on the show.

That bit of drama was the least of it. I only had two episodes in which to shake things up but if that was my job then things were well and truly shaken.

Of course, I completely ignored the rule about not getting off with any of the girls.

Neither was that the only rule that I tore up. On the last evening, I grabbed a bottle of champagne and refused to leave the villa and go back to my digs. I'd gone from seeing myself as playing a part to getting a bit carried away with everything. I was given so much free rein and looking back I can see I didn't necessarily use it in the best possible way. To be honest, I'd lost sight of myself a bit then. I'd stopped caring. I was earning my bad boy reputation and playing up to it at the same time.

I was also, let's face it, seeing through it all. Seeing it for the entertainment creation that it really was. Like, some guy who meets a girl two days ago, says she's now his girlfriend, and then gets angry when she kisses someone else. I mean, really? Come on. He's only known her five minutes. Everybody talking about each other behind their backs. Contestants snitching on each other.

Me, if I'm gonna say something about somebody, then I'll say it to their face. That was my point of difference with the other cast members. Most of them didn't have the cahones to say to each other what they were saying behind their backs. I did. Not because I'm super tough, just because I had the balls to do it. I knew what these people were like. I knew they didn't give a shit about me or even really about themselves. They were just acting on TV.

When you have that knowledge, you feel a kind of freedom. It makes you feel like you can do anything. It gives you a kind of power that the others don't have.

As a result, I looked strong, and because I looked strong there was conflict, and conflict is what the production needs.

Which is not to say that I was a complete nightmare. I don't want you to get the wrong impression, because one thing about me is that I'm really friendly. I get on with anyone. I used to flirt with the dinner ladies at school; like if I went on a date with someone on *Ex on the Beach* then I'd get on with them, whether I fancied them or not. I was friendly and nice with people I met on the PAs. And I swear to God that's as much a side of me as the hot-headedness is. If I say that I played up to my reputation on the show, well, maybe a little bit, with some drink inside me, it was still me. I never stopped being me. I never stopped projecting myself.

People ask me if I look back now and recognise that guy causing havoc. Do I recognise that guy as the same guy who looks back at me from the mirror now, in 2023, having been through everything that I've been through, having lost my little girl to a cruel disease?

The answer is yes and no. The confrontational side of me, in terms of staying true to myself and standing up for what I believe in, is still there. But the main difference between me and that guy is that something happened, and it happened because of Azaylia.

What happened was that I gained purpose. And the gaining of that purpose has meant that I took all of the good things about me, and maybe reframed some of the bad things, and channelled them into becoming the person I am now, which is the person who works to honour my daughter's memory. It's age. It's maturity. But more than that, it's purpose.

In the meantime, the wagon train would keep on rolling as soon as season two of *Ex on the Beach* was broadcast, but there was still a bit of a lull between the excitement from season one tailing off and that one kicking into gear.

Once again, that left me casting around for something to do. At the same time, I was looking for new management and ended up going with a mate who was just starting out in the game.

The fit seemed good. By this stage, I had a large social media profile, and was looking for ways to capitalise on that. My new manager, DMO also managed a DJ called DJ Russke, who used to release sets on SoundCloud and Mixcloud at the time, so I learned how to DJ and asked my manager to look for bookings.

Next thing you know, I'm 'Ex on the Beach star Ashley Cain, DJ', which gave me this extra bit of longevity before season two appeared. Pretty soon, I was DJing all over the show: appearing at clubs in London, Manchester and Newcastle, as well as abroad. I DJed every week in Malia and Zante and did guest sets in Valencia, Ayia Napa, Pisa, Dubai, Marbella, and Amsterdam. I'd end up doing a whole tour, six weeks in Australia: limos, flights, hotels, the works.

When the second season of Ex on the Beach appeared it was like shovelling more coal onto the fire. I was getting hotter and hotter.

Around this time I was going out with a girl from Essex. Usually I had a bit of an entourage when I'd go DJing in clubs, turning up with about eight, nine, ten mates. This one time, however, it was just me, her and her mates.

I'd DJed and then was hanging afterwards, when three guys came to our table, big dudes. Me, I was gym big. They were naturally big. We got talking, kind of bantering, a little bit friendly, a little bit competitive, the way it sometimes goes down, before one of them challenged me to an arm-wrestle.

Arm-wrestling. This was right up my street. My dad sometimes took me out with him when I was fourteen; he would put money down on me beating blokes at arm wrestling and he rarely lost. I was pretty good at it.

This night, however, I was drunk, I was with my girlfriend and her mates, and I didn't want to arm-wrestle. I could see the way the evening might go: three guys looking not for a fight necessarily, but to prove themselves; me with six girls. The dynamic was all wrong.

Still, though, the guys were insistent, and it was better to arm-wrestle than to scrap.

Okay, fine. Whatever. Let's arm-wrestle.

Now, when you arm-wrestle, you put your arm in, you twist your wrist and you lock your arm with your shoulder. Using your body. That's the key. You think it's all in the arms, but it's not. It's in the shoulder through the body.

On this occasion, and for reasons that escape me, probably to do with the amount I'd had to drink, I decided to do things differently. I put my arm out and held it there. I thought to myself, I'm stronger than him and I've got more willpower. I'm just going to hold him like that. I'm going to hold him, wear him out and win that way.

We go at it. Me with my frankly barmy new approach to arm-wrestling. Him not wanting to lose face in front of his mates or the girls. That was how it stayed for a while. How long, I'm not sure. All I remember is that suddenly there was …

Bang.

Yes, yes. Yet another bang. At first I thought that one of his mates had punched me. I was literally going, 'Who hit me? Who the fuck hit me?' And then I looked around and could see the girls shrinking away, the guy I was arm-wrestling holding his hands up, other people in the club looking across at me, their faces like they'd seen something bad, really bad.

Which of course they had.

They were seeing the fact that my arm had …

Flopped.

I was wearing a long-sleeved top at the time, but under the sleeve, my arm looked like it was hanging off.

It would later turn out that I had a clean break and spiral fracture down both sides of the broken bone.

I cradled my arm to my chest. My girlfriend was insisting I go to the hospital, but there was a house party going on, and I wanted to attend. We went along and partied for the rest of the night, with me just sort of holding my arm as I waited for it to get better.

But of course it didn't get better. As the adrenaline and the booze wore off, it got worse, a lot worse, until my other half was insisting – and for once I was agreeing with her – that we needed to get to the hospital.

The long and the short of it was that I ended up having an operation during which I had my whole humerus plated and pinned together, and while that healed, they fitted me with a cast.

It wouldn't have been so bad, except that I was booked to go on season five of *Ex on the Beach*.

CHAPTER 23

Being invited back to *Ex on the Beach* was pretty special for me. It was an all-stars edition they were touting as a season where previous cast members who had 'unfinished business' would return in order to get, I don't know, 'closure' or something. It was being filmed at Koh Samui in Thailand.

Either way, it was pretty exciting to go back for a third season. And it wouldn't be like season two, where I'd been parachuted in towards the end of the run. This time I'd be appearing from episode three onwards.

I've always been really into my gear. I'd wear loud clothes. When I became a pro footballer, I deviated from the usual trainee role, which is that the youngsters keep their heads down, don't stand out. But that's not me and I'm unapologetic about that.

So when I went on the first season of *Ex on the Beach*, I'd worn gold shorts, gold chains, gold sunglasses. I carried a gold rucksack. I was literally all gold. And for my season five re-entry, the production took my gold theme and ran with it. They gave me gold shorts and – wait for it – a gold crown and gold cape, and I made my entrance on top of the villa.

Why?

Because I was being billed as – wait for it – 'King of the Villa'.

But there was a small problem. Actually, there were two small problems.

The first was the fact that I had a gammy arm.

The second was that I hadn't told my girlfriend I was going back on the show.

Funnily enough, when the offer first came through, I was very much in two minds whether I should take it up, precisely because I had this great relationship that I didn't want to endanger. On the other hand, excuse the pun, there was the issue of my arm. Being out of action I hadn't been able to play football or DJ, which had limited my earning opportunities. Going on the show meant a welcome injection of cash.

I wasn't supposed to fly with my arm in that condition, plus I was pretty sure that if I came clean, the production team would have barred me from appearing, and so I kept schtum about it, the result being that I ended up filming all of season five of *Ex on the Beach* with an arm that was way, way below fully functional – and nobody knew a thing about it.

Not an easy task. If you've seen *Ex on the Beach*, then you'll know that it's not like I could hide my injury under a big sweatshirt. The boys on the show very rarely wear shirts so I had no choice but to bare all. To this day I have a long scar running down my right arm, but at the time it was especially visible. The same arm was also much less pumped than the other, although watching it back now, it doesn't actually look too bad. I mean, to my eyes it literally looked weak and withered, but I accept that you can't really tell on camera.

Arm-wise, the worst moment came the day we had to go to the Pink Elephant waterpark, which has a ride they call the Super Bowl, a huge bowl slide. You drop about ten people into this fishbowl, and they swish round and round and round before dropping into the water. The production were going, 'We need this scene, we need this scene,' and I was saying, 'No, I don't want to do it like that,' desperately trying not to let on how bad my arm was.

'Why not? Come on Ash ...'

They're thinking, *WFT. This is the so-called 'bad boy of MTV'. How come he's such a wuss all of a sudden?*

I was thinking, *Oh God, oh God, oh God.* I had to do it whether I liked it or not, even at the risk of snapping my arm. And so I did, and for once there was no *bang*, and my arm stayed in one piece.

Gaz – that's Gary Beadle from *Geordie Shore*, who was also in season two with me – was on the show. So was Chloe Goodman, a glamour model who was in the first season, as was Liam Lewis. Kayleigh Morris, who was one of the second season cast members and my ex, was there, while Jess Impiazzi and Melissa Reeves also came back from season two. We also had Jemma Lucy and Stephen Bear.

Even with my broken arm, I wanted to be the alpha dog. There are lots of similarities between school and going on a reality show (it probably won't surprise you to learn) but as far as I was concerned the main one was never to show weakness.

If you show weakness, that's when they pounce. You know what I mean, right? If there's an injured lion in the pride, it's finished. If you're in a fight and you're limping, your opponent will take aim at the wounded leg.

(Don't get me wrong, I'm not saying that you should never show vulnerability, because I don't think that anybody who's seen me cry over the passing of my daughter would ever think I'm weak. They know that from that place of pain comes strength and the will to fight for change. It's important to recognise that.)

I got a lot from *Ex on the Beach*. Having appeared on three seasons, I was no longer just that year's 'thing', I was a bit of a fixture.

But.

Big but. *Ex on the Beach* was big but it was no *TOWIE*, where pretty much every cast member has gone on to other things. It was no *Made in Chelsea*, no *Geordie Shore*. And like all of those shows, it had reached the apex of its popularity. It had peaked.

So, the question for me was, 'What next?'

CHAPTER 24

A while after season five of *Ex on the Beach*, I was invited to a Tom Zanetti music video shoot where I met Chloe Khan, who had been on *Snog, Marry, Avoid* and also *The X Factor*, where she'd appeared as Chloe Mafia, as well as going on to be a *Playboy* bunny.

In reality-TV terms, she was a pretty big star at the time, had millions of followers on social media and was doing very well financially.

I was doing my thing at the shoot, just bouncing around, being like Tigger and getting on with everybody, maybe surprising a few folk that I wasn't at all like my bad boy image in the flesh, and I ended up hitting it off with Chloe.

She and I went out that night, had a lot of fun and both posted a picture that we took of ourselves in the club. The next day it was in the papers that Ashley Cain and Chloe Khan were an item, and we kind of agreed that we were. We fancied each other, we got on well, so …

Chloe was great. I get that she's divisive, and that half of the people you ask seem to hate her while the other half love her, but actually she's a really, really sound person. She was nice, she'd do things for you, she'd want to see you all the time and she was fun when you were with her. It felt different to other relationships. And when I DJ'ed, she came along and we'd make a night of it.

The problem was that our relationship became like another TV show, because we'd be in the papers every week. You know how I was saying that celebs contact the paps? Well, that was how I found out, because Chloe would call 'her pap' in order to get us in the papers every week.

It got mad, and it wasn't quite my thing. But it certainly wasn't enough to put me off Chloe, and the relationship got to the point where we were making plans to move in together, actually looking at houses.

Stuff happened. Not stuff I want to go into here, because it's private, but we got over it – mainly because she was so cool about some stupid shit that I did – and the relationship carried on.

But something within me had changed. Or should I say *was changing*. You might simply call it maturity. You might call it something else. Either way it was the building blocks of the person I am today, and it began as the appeal of nightlife began to wane. Falling drunk out of places in the early hours, having my picture taken, all that kind of stuff. The novelty was wearing off.

It wasn't that I didn't want to go out any more. Just that I could take it or leave it. I stopped enjoying going to all these events. Hanging out at parties didn't seem so attractive any more. I was no longer arsed about getting my picture taken all the time.

I'd also realised that I wanted my relationship to be separate from what you might say was my professional life, which was ironic, because before Chloe my girlfriends had often given me hassle about the media side of what I did, like they didn't really understand it.

Then I get a woman who's completely fine with it, and suddenly I decide that I don't want a public relationship. And with us, the more serious it got, the more public it seemed to get.

Look, I'm not gonna complain. Nor am I knocking anyone who's into that life. If that was Chloe's bag, fine. It just wasn't mine any more. When I had the appetite for it, I had a great time.

Just that I no longer wanted it.

The good thing was that the whole time I was out polishing up my bad-boy-party-animal legend status – and some of the stories, man, I could fill a whole book with them, but that's not why we are here – I was still training, still going to the gym, still keeping healthy.

As a result, gym brands were interested and I got sponsorship that way. I started doing a bit of modelling; I'd be going to events and I was working hard. It wasn't as though the Ashley Cain you now know had just appeared, fully fledged – it took Azaylia for that to happen – but he was starting to make his presence felt.

I remember once pulling into the car park of the gym, maybe one Monday morning with a really sore head, and it was like a light went off in my head. I thought to myself, *Where has the last four years gone? What have you done with this precious gift of life?*

This was the problem. You talk about going out and having a good time, but how good a time are you having when you can't even remember it the next day? People forget that about booze. It turns every unique experience into the same experience. It takes everything that should be special and memorable and kind of blurs it out into a muddy generic whole. And what's the point in that? I felt like a wreck-head. I felt as though I had no future.

I'm not proud of my behaviour at the end of my relationship with Chloe, but I suppose you'd have to say that I ghosted her. She got in touch saying the press had contacted her, wanting to know whether we were on or off, and I told her, 'Just say what you want.' The fact was, we were no longer an item.

After she and I split, I did an E4 show called *Five-Star Hotel*. By then, I was well and truly disillusioned with the whole night-life, celebrity-circus side of things. The idea of the show was that me, Joey Essex and Spencer Matthews from *Made in Chelsea*, Olivia from *The Only Way Is Essex*, and Holly from *Geordie Shore* had to run a hotel in Greece.

Five-Star Hotel was one of the funniest shows I've ever done. Normally when you do reality TV – certainly all the shows I've ever been on – you're in a villa or a complex. You have fixed-rig cameras and occasionally they wheel out a crew, but whatever happens, you belong to the production team: you have no phone; there's no break from filming; you can't leave if you want, unless you want to make a big deal of it; you eat when they give you food; the lights go on when they want them to go on; the lights go off when they want them to go off; you consume alcohol when they want you to, and they take all of that stuff away when it suits them.

In short, you're a slave to the production team, and the production team is a slave to content and that's it. Being on the show, you start to understand the way they work. Like, if there's been drama during the day then they don't give you alcohol. This might be because they feel they already have enough material, or maybe it's because they don't want to inflame the situation, maybe some combination of the two.

But of course the opposite is also true. If there hasn't been much going on during the day, then they give you alcohol. And if the alcohol provokes a bit of drama, then they swoop in and take it away.

Saying all that, *Five-Star Hotel* was just a different thing altogether. The idea was that me and the others would be the five 'stars' who were running a hotel on the Greek island of Eos. We got to keep our phones. The guests coming in? They were the cattle this time around. They were being treated the way we used to get treated on *Ex on the Beach*.

Eos was a tiny little place. You had to fly into Mykonos and get a ferry across. What we soon discovered was that it was full of Australians and a bit crazy. The show itself was great, though. The idea was that the celebs (i.e. us) would run the hotel and compete to win Employee of the Season. It probably would have been even better if I hadn't ended up getting the boot first. Like, by the end of the second episode I'd been given an official warning because I'd slept with one of the guests, and I continued playing to type. And then I got the boot.

There were bits and pieces that happened behind the scenes

as well, which probably didn't help matters. Things were getting a bit fractious, let's say. None of it was broadcast.

That's the funny thing about doing a reality show. You're filmed twenty-four hours a day and it's boiled down to forty-two minutes of an episode. As you're bowling around making the programme, things happen and you say to yourself, *I bet that'll be in the show,* but inevitably you're wrong. Obviously, the production team know their business and perhaps there are certain things they simply cannot show for whatever reason, but their choices never fail to surprise me.

That's part of the reason I used to think it was so mad that people would be acting up for the cameras. What's the point? Chances are none of it will get shown anyway. Might as well just save yourself a lot of bother and be yourself.

For me, *Five-Star Hotel* was just business as usual. After all, that's why I was there. More or less. You get some contestants who are Goody Two-Shoes and do everything by the book. You get some contestants who act out. That's just the way it is. Producers like them both but for different reasons. I never thought of it as being behaviour that might threaten my future chances or endanger my career. It was what it was.

Little did I know, however, that my life was about to take another major turn. I was going to meet Saf.

CHAPTER 25

There was a bit of inaccuracy in the last sentence of that chapter. I didn't 'meet' Saf at that point. In actual fact, I already knew Saf and had known her since I was sixteen or seventeen. Like me, she was from the Nuneaton area and in fact, owned a salon there. Just that while I recognised her from around, I didn't really know her. It was more that I was on nodding-saying-hello terms with her.

But the relationship kicked into another gear when we were on a night out with separate groups of mates who nevertheless knew each other – it was either Coventry or Birmingham – and found ourselves sitting together.

We got talking and one of the things that first struck me – something I really liked – was how easy she was to be around. I thought she was cool, funny, open-minded, and I instantly took to her in a way I hadn't with anybody else before. A couple of years later, and I'd be wanting to have children with Saf. I'd think of her as 'the one' in a way that I never had with previous girlfriends. I'm not saying I knew that right away, just that the seeds were sown.

It was lucky that meeting up with her came at the same time that I was having my reflective moments, wondering what I was doing and where I was going with my life. Being from round the way, Saf was not part of the old me, the reality TV star me. There was an irony there: she was a face from back in the day, and yet she also represented something new. I liked that she had no airs and graces. I loved how she didn't take herself too seriously. She enjoyed having a laugh more than she liked being cool, if that makes sense. She wasn't afraid of looking silly.

That night we exchanged numbers, pretty soon we were meeting up. And because she was so close, we would get together frequently. I really fancied her, no doubt about that, but we met up as friends, initially in groups with other mates, and then just the two of us. They weren't dates; they were more like outings. The cinema, stuff like that. It was nice.

Because she caught me during 'the change', I took things slow with her. The old me was fast. Proper hunter-gatherer stuff. New me? Not so much. I was redefining what it meant to be a man. Where before I'd thought it meant catting around, having a new girl every night, that wasn't me any more. I wanted to care for somebody. I wanted someone to care for me. So with Saf, I was being …

Well, I wasn't being anything. I was just being me. Just a new version of me. But maybe the new version of me was slightly at odds with my image or the way I came across, because after a while she was was like, 'Yo, do you like me or not?'

That was the thing. That was why I was giving her all this space. Yes, I liked her. With Saf, I wasn't just in love with her looks or her sex appeal, although she had bags of both. I loved her personality. I loved spending time with her. It was one of those relationships where we'd spend the day together, and then the night together, and that would turn into two days together, which would turn into three, which would turn into a whole week.

She had no public profile, which was a plus point as far as I was concerned. Before her, I either went out with girls who had a profile, who probably enjoyed the publicity too much for my liking. Or I went out with girls who didn't have a profile but had a problem with mine. She was neither of those.

And do you know what else? Saf didn't judge me. I think that feeling of being judged was a large part of why I felt that I had to change. I felt like I'd been judged my whole life. At school, in football, even on TV. And that maybe a percentage of people who stood in judgement were also looking down on me, perhaps even trying to mess with my life and make a mess of my head.

I know the way it goes. You look at me, you see muscles, tattoos, the hair and the beard. You're going to reach your own conclusions. Maybe even jump to those conclusions, yeah? The number of times I've met people and they've said, 'You know what? You're actually a really nice guy.' I thank them for that, but even so, I think, *Yeah. Maybe next time reserve your judgement until after you've met me.*

But Saf, who had seen me on TV and knew of my reputation, had done exactly that. She'd waited until she knew me to decide whether she liked me. And I'm happy to say that she decided she did.

It was some months after we became a couple that we decided to begin living together. She wasn't the first girl I'd ever lived with, but definitely the first who was on equal terms. Before, it had been like one of us had moved into the other's place. Saf was the first girl where we'd have a shared place together. It marked a bit of an upturn in my overall fortunes as well. The little deals and hustles I was doing turned into slightly bigger deals and hustles and Saf was a huge help, just as I was a big support with her beauty business.

We were a proper team then. Mutually supportive, getting our business shit together, going out and having lots of fun. I'm not gonna lie, it was a really, really great time.

I guess the one blot on the horizon was the fact that I had another show coming up. This one was *The Challenge*.

CHAPTER 26

A time like that – like I was having with Saf then – tells you something about your life. It tells you how you can turn things around. I've always been lucky enough to have had brilliant, strong and supportive people around me. If you've read this far, you'll already know that: my dad with his tough love; my mum with her nurturing and caring kind of love. My doting grandparents, my siblings, my auntie … in fact, my whole family. And then Saf.

Then, of course, Azaylia.

Collectively, these people have been my rock, often without really knowing it, because one of the things about me is that I don't tend to let people – not even the ones closest to me – know how I'm feeling. My life has always been very inconsistent. At the point I'm talking about now, I started to make money, and that was great, not just from a personal point of view, and the fact that I could provide for Saf, and later for Azaylia, but also from a family point of view, because one thing about our family is that we've always tried to do better than the generation that came before. It's what we strive for.

But that making-money time came after a life of great inconsistency. I tend to say that I've always been more broke than I've had money. I'll always say that I've had more pain than I've had pleasure. That things have gone more against me than they have for me. And yet the crazy flipside of that is that I always get people who say things like, 'It's all right for you …' Because they see that I've got money.

And I have, I'm not gonna lie. I was doing well then, and I'm doing well now. I've filmed multiple shows. I present on TV. I have my own podcast. I have sponsorship deals, I'm a sponsored athlete and have my own show with MTV. But the main thing is, no matter what I do, it has to align with my beliefs. It has to motivate, inspire, evoke positivity and help people. That's how I choose what I do. And the fact is that I turn away way more work and money than I take because it isn't right morally for me and doesn't align with my purpose.

I'm not saying this to brag. I'm saying this because it's the truth. I'm saying it because the people who claim, 'It's all right for you …' don't realise that I don't come from that place of money. I come from modest circumstances. I've been penniless and in dark places, thanks to the bad luck I've had. But here's the thing: I didn't let on. Even though I believe wholeheartedly that you should talk through your problems, and that bottling them up is the wrong thing to do, I always knew that in order to create opportunity, I needed to maintain a positive mindset.

Through that I was always determined that I should never be the victim. Right from that shitty time at school, I was determined to turn the negative into a positive. If I had to run to a job interview, it was because I wanted to get fit, not because I couldn't afford the petrol. That's the way I span it. When I went to see the guy about the e-cigarettes, I didn't let the fact that I didn't have money hold me back. I had an idea. I had a contacts book. I had vision.

And now? Now that things have changed even more?

Well, we'll come on to that.

The fact was that for the time being, things were great. Just that there was this *The Challenge* show to navigate.

The approach was from MTV USA, which, as you can imagine, is big. Not only that, but *The Challenge* is a massive show for them. How big are we talking? We are talking billboards in Times Square. That's how big.

The show had started life as a spin-off from MTV's other reality shows, *The Real World*, and *Road Rules*, and featured cast members from those two shows. When it was first broadcast, in 1998, it had been called *Road Rules: All-Stars*, but then was renamed something else, and then by the time of the nineteenth season, when it featured cast members from a variety of other reality shows, it was called *The Challenge*.

Ours was the thirty-third season. And like the others it had a subtitle: *War of the Worlds*, the idea being that contestants hailing from a number of different countries would be taking on 'America's best'. On it would be cast members from *The Real World, The Bachelor, Big Brother, Celebrity Big Brother UK, Love Island UK, Geordie Shore* ... you name it.

But of course, the offer came at the wrong time. I had just moved in with Saf. I wanted to settle down and create a life together. I was not 'that guy' any more. I was a changed man. The thing about *War of the Worlds* was that we would all be living together, just as we were in *Ex on the Beach*, except with the addition of the most insane live challenges you can possibly imagine. I was thinking, *There's got to be a reason why you want me on this show.* I knew the way their minds worked. I knew the way reality TV was structured. Everyone's got their roles, haven't they? You look at something like, for example, *Dancing on Ice*, or even *Strictly Come Dancing*, you've got some people in there for what is basically comedy value, other people who are primed to go the distance and possibly win. People bring to the table their own distinct personalities.

What did they want from me? No prizes for guessing. They wanted the bad boy. They wanted the short fuse and the even shorter temper.

Saf was always really supportive of what I did and do, but she was, understandably, not too keen. Come on, I was going to be away for eight weeks, massively adrenalised, playing up to the cameras and with a reputation for doing the business on reality shows. Well, you wouldn't be keen, would you?

As a result, I thought about not going, but part of being a changed man had involved giving up the DJing. So that was one revenue stream lost to me. Nor was I blind to the fact that my continued prosperity relied at least in part on me continuing to have a public profile. I mean, look, there's no point in pretending otherwise: it was too big an opportunity to pass up.

The game itself involved sixteen *Challenge* 'veterans' and then eighteen what they call 'prospects', who were new *Challenge* competitors from all around the world. And by 'all around the world', I mean the UK, Brazil and Turkey.

I was one of several Brits on the show. Others were Stephen

Bear, Theo Campbell from *Love Island*, Kyle Christie and Zahida Allen from *Geordie Shore*, and Georgia Harrison from *TOWIE*. And what we Brits didn't realise was how seriously the Americans take it all. I think it's fair to say that we were there for a bit of a laugh. It was, after all, just a TV show, and the challenges while being super tough to complete, of course – otherwise it wouldn't be worth doing – were still just TV challenges. They're still being conceived, staged, filmed and broadcast for one reason and one reason only, and that's entertainment. I'm not saying you needed to be a reality TV veteran to know that. I'm not even saying that you needed to be a Brit to know that. Just that it panned out that way: the American contestants took it very, very seriously indeed. Us lot? Not so much.

I mean, I had the Americans telling me stories about how they had been training for months beforehand, one or two hours a day, just to get ready for the show. There were contestants who had taken to walking around their houses blindfold in order to become accustomed to the 'blind' challenges. Others who had gone on something called a Ninja Warrior course. And there was us thinking this was a normal reality TV show. There was us thinking we'd have a bit of a laugh. It's not that we didn't take it seriously or that we disrespected the brand, or MTV, or anything like that, just that – how shall I put it? – it was as though we felt like we were more aware of why we were really there than the others.

After a 'Basic Training' episode, the proper show began. First came the business of choosing a partner. Each prospect had to team up with a veteran of the opposite sex, and that was decided by an opening challenge game.

Two of the two lowest-ranking prospects were eliminated. The rest of us chose our partners with yours truly as the winner picking first. My choice? Kam Williams, who had originally appeared on a US reality show called *Are You the One?* before really making a name for herself on *The Challenge*, where she had gained the nickname 'Killa Kam'. Why, you ask, was she called 'Killa Kam'? Good question. Reason being that she was one of the best players when it came to the elimination round of the contest.

Which brings us on to the next stage of the game. Now we'd picked our teams, the real meat of the show kicked in. For each round, each round being one episode, there would be a daily mission where every pair competes in the daily challenge.

The first of the challenge games was called 'Arms-A-Geddon Tired'; we basically had to play a big tug-of-war game. Me and Kam missed out on a top-three place but lived to fight another round.

And that's where the shit hit the fan for me. This round was called 'Search and Destroy' and was played in four heats. The idea was to find a hidden ball in a graveyard and return it to your partner, who then had to take the ball through a mud pit, avoiding other competitors to reach the safe zone.

So the first challenge came around where the two teams had to retrieve balls, the number of which would be reduced for each round. There I was taking part in this round, running around the graveyard, doing my best when guess what?

That's right.

Bang.

Hamstring gone. I had torn it.

With great difficulty, I made it through and won the

challenge. But I had the whole of the rest of the show to do. Plus, if (and when) it got out that I had a torn hamstring, I would be laser targeted by my fellow contestants.

For both of the next two games, my torn hamstring prevented us getting in the top three, but we stayed safe from the tribunal. I think that people didn't want to face me and Kam in elimination because we had strong ties on both the UK and US sides, and most eliminations were head-to-head physical challenges. That was until the 'Eye in the Sky' challenge, where we ended up being in the tribunal pick and were then called out, meaning we had to face Amanda and Josh in a challenge called 'Uphill Battle'. We won that one. Lived to fight another day.

Meanwhile, there were of course some of the usual shenanigans – but I really felt like, at this point, people were seeing a changed version of me. There were a couple of guys there who I rubbed up the wrong way and vice versa – I think people were used to that hot-headed version of me, and it wasn't easy to keep a cool head all the time (as some of you will know if you watched it).

I ended up being out there for four weeks. Which was not as long as the eight weeks it might have been, of course, but that suited me fine. I had done what I needed to do, and I could jet home back to Saf.

When I got home, life continued as normal and I guess at some point, Saf and I had a conversation about children, which I reckon is where 'we' came in …

Part Four

LION

CHAPTER 27

Cast your mind back to when I was sitting beside my brother Matty, both of us holding our little girls and getting our picture taken, with me feeling as though a new chapter in my life had begun. Feeling like ...

Oh, *everything*. Up until that point, I'd always hustled and bustled, and if there's one word that describes my life up until then, what with all the shit that had gone down during my childhood, my football, being on TV, and various relationships, that word would be 'colourful'.

And yet, sitting there holding Azaylia, I was struck by a sense that in fact the opposite was true. That my life, while not exactly black and white, had been a kind of sepia, and now it was as though somebody had turned the colour up. Everything went full-colour bright.

I looked at her and thought she was beautiful, and that with her in it, the world was suddenly beautiful, too. Everything looked bright. The walls. The way the sun bounced off the pavement. Where before my thoughts had always been of myself and how I was going to make money, how I needed to work out or whatever. Now my thoughts were of Azaylia.

And it wasn't just a fleeting thing either. I mean, I guess this book is about a variety of things, Azaylia mainly. But tied into that is a story of change. During the time between the end of my relationship with Chloe and the beginning of my relationship with Saf, my period of growth was something that happened quite gradually. It was a process of creeping realisation. But in the days and weeks following Azaylia's birth, this profound change was something that happened suddenly. It was like a bomb – a kaleidoscopic, multicoloured bomb – had detonated in the middle of my life, awakening me, bringing light to where there had been greyness.

Now I went out into the world and my thought processes were different. As I bopped around with a new-dad spring in my step, I looked at the world through new eyes and saw how different it all was, how everything glistened and shone, even the bricks, and how all the doubt and uncertainty that had enveloped me like a shroud seemed to fall away: the countless injuries, the money worries, the relationship woes. All of it faded into the distance, and I thought to myself, *I'm all right. I'm safe. I'm stable. Life is beautiful.*

Looking back, I was twenty-nine and it was the first time I knew exactly who I was and just who I needed to be. In doing so, I learned a lesson that I've lived by ever since, and live by now: that if you make life about you, you'll never be happy. You need to make your life about other people.

It was in gazing at Azaylia, thinking about her and about Saf, that I finally found some meaning.

Didn't even know I was looking for it. Didn't even know it was there.

Not until I found it.

The wonderful thing about that first period with Azaylia, when everything seemed all right with the world, when the word 'cancer' had not yet become a part of our lives, was that Saf and I learned about raising a child together. We'd be educating ourselves as we went along, and as had always been the case with me and her, having fun, enjoying ourselves.

Saf was really quite cool and laidback. Me, I'm what you might call a thinker, maybe an overthinker. I like to be able to explain things. I like to rationalise. With a kid, though, a precious tiny being, there is no explanation, no rationalisation. It just is what it is.

It's magic. It's love.

And you can't stop yourself from kissing her, wanting to bury your nose in her hair. You just can't stop yourself.

She was a healthy baby, that was the thing. A tiny, healthy, blue-eyed little thing with her parents' ethnicities having combined to give her the most delicious colouring you can possibly imagine. She had a cherubic face and tiny lips like petals. To me, she looked small, so unbelievably small. She'd been born a healthy weight of 7 lb, but I could hold her along my arm and I could enclose her foot in one of my fists.

Imagine that! Imagine being so small that someone can hold one of your tiny feet in their fingertips. Imagine being picked up and carried around by loving giants whose only job is to keep you safe. Perhaps that's why we don't remember life as babies, because we'd mourn that time so much if we did.

We'd grieve for a time when our parents had no job other than looking after and loving us.

Again, you can't explain that. Try rationalising that. It's impossible.

So instead you do what I did, which was to happily, joyfully surrender myself to the business of being a new dad.

And God, I loved it.

She wasn't a great sleeper, not that we cared. We evolved into an ecosystem of three. If Azaylia needed our attention then she got it, whatever the time of day or night. Now, I know that some people find the whole sleep thing a real problem, and I'm not judging them. And I know couples argue about who's going to get up or whatever, but that wasn't us. Not because we were Goody Two-Shoes, hashtag best parents in the world, or any of that shit. Just because that's the way we were.

'Shall I go?'

'Don't worry about it, babe, I'll go.'

'You went last night.'

'Yeah, don't worry. I'll go tonight, it doesn't matter.'

I know. Finger-down-the-throat time. But I'm not gonna lie, it's just how it was. It's like Azaylia would wake you up in the middle of the night and instead of feeling like you were being robbed of sleep, it would simply be a great excuse to see her, entertain her, play with her. Just to *be* with Azaylia.

It was around this time that I started singing and dancing with her. Saf's got a video on her phone that features me grooving along to a song that she can no longer listen to, 'Go Crazy' by Chris Brown. Azaylia would be crying in her cot, which was by the side of the bed, as it was from the day she came home. She'd wake up, as babies do, and I'd go to her, pick her up, and start singing Chris Brown.

We had a midwife visit, of course. A Covid-compliant midwife. Azaylia was given a clean bill of health, the only problem being that she was a bit bunged up. You could tell that from her breathing. We were given a small bulb syringe designed to suck the mucus from her nose, although Grandma Cain took one look at it and said, "Bwoi, you don't put that in a baby, man. Put your mouth on her nose, suck it up, man, suck it up.'

Yeah, probably a Caribbean thing. But it didn't bother me. I went ahead and sucked the snot out of Azaylia's nose, although because I was a panicky parent (well, according to Saf), I was terrified of sucking too hard. My grandma may have been outraged at the sight of the bulb syringe, but at least you know where you are with one of those. You don't have to worry about accidentally sucking out your baby's brains.

So anyway, that's what we did. As advised.

But then Saf's intuition kicked in.

'Something's not right,' she said.

CHAPTER 28

A few weeks in, there were even more things which began to worry us. Azaylia had been such a restful little one, but now she was unsettled. I was singing Chris Brown more regularly, and it wasn't having much effect.

Thanks to the pandemic, we were in the era of telephone consultations only, so Saf got on the phone and was told that it might be a feeding issue. Perhaps Azaylia was hungry. In response, we increased her feeds, topping up Saf's breast milk with formula.

In addition to the restlessness, the stuffiness wasn't easing, and in fact seemed to be getting worse. Azaylia had moved from being 'a bit bunged up' to really quite seriously congested and was now exhibiting cold and flu symptoms.

There was something else too. Something even more worrying.

Her belly had started to get a little bloated. Added to which it didn't feel quite right: it felt a little hard.

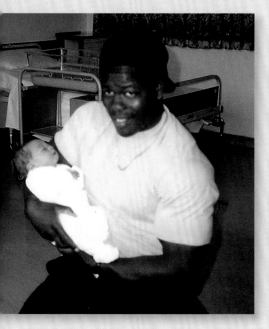

My parents, Anthony and Vicky, were brilliant. The Cain household was always a very happy one.

As a cheeky little kid, I was very active from an early age. I loved sport but school slightly less so . . . I was always pushing boundaries and testing my limits.

From my days on the football pitch to the nation's screens on reality TV, it's been one hell of a ride. But by far my greatest achievement and adventure was becoming a father.

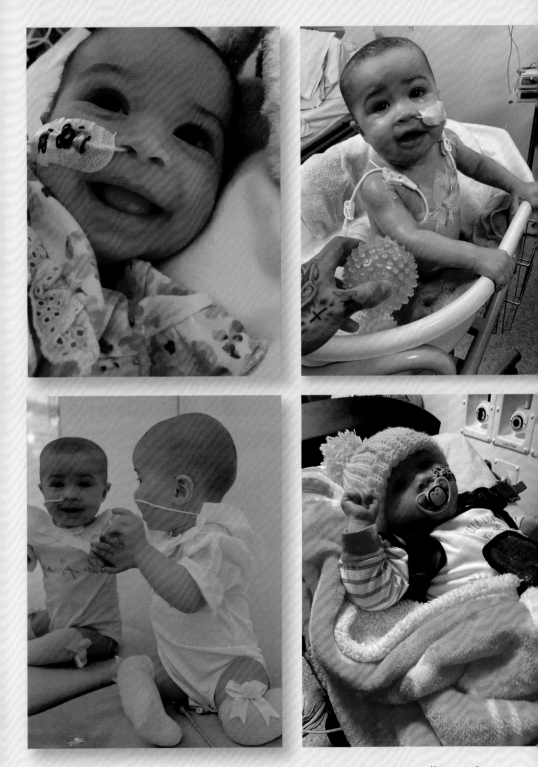

The days, weeks and months after Azaylia's diagnosis were really tough. But, despite the many tests and Azaylia's needs increasing, Club 100 remained a positive space. Azaylia was the most beautiful, smiley, little girl. Even when things were at their hardest, she gave me courage.

Saf and I decided that we would do everything in our power to make Azaylia's time in hospital as happy as we possibly could.

Above and left: We made sure we were involved in the festivities around Halloween and Christmas, celebrating with the other children on Ward 18.

Right: Ringing the bell at the end of Azaylia's treatment was a very emotional day. Despite her prognosis, I am glad that my brave little girl got to ring the bell to celebrate everything she had achieved.

Azaylia's days at home were so important to us. We surrounded her with as much love and care as possible. Our families were hugely important in supporting us during this time and I am so grateful to everyone who was present in her last days.

Right: As we didn't have to be so careful about the risk of germs, I had the chance to take Azaylia out for walks. Being able to spend time with her outside the confines of a hospital room meant everything to me.

Left: One of the most special moments during this time was Azaylia meeting her cousin, Anaya, again. When their hands touched, I felt like my heart might break, but that moment will stay with me for my lifetime.

Azaylia and her smile touched people around the world. Her strength and bravery captured the hearts of so many.

Right: A few days before her passing there was a flypast over our house, spelling out 'A' for Azaylia.

Below: Azaylia's Day will stay with me forever. No parent ever imagines they will be present at the funeral of their child, but we ensured that this day would honour the impact Azaylia had, not just on our lives, but upon anyone who had witnessed her story.

From cycling, to running, to kayaking, there is no challenge I will not undertake, no mountain I will not climb in order to keep spreading awareness of the fight against childhood cancer. Through these challenges, not only do I raise money for this vital cause, but I get the chance to take Azaylia with me across the world, every step of the way.

When all is said and done, the miles travelled and the money raised is all down to this special little girl. She is the reason I will never rest, she is the reason I stay true to my cause in raising awareness for the fight against childhood cancer.

Azaylia Diamond Cain, my angel.

Saf rang for another phone consultation, describing the symptoms. We were told that constipation was the most likely cause, recommended some laxatives and told to rub her belly and pump her legs, in order to encourage a bowel movement.

At this stage we were concerned enough to ring the doctor but not quite worried enough to panic. We knew that babies are prone to all kinds of little things when they're new, but also that they're pretty robust when all is said and done.

And yet ...

And yet the bunged-up thing wasn't going, and was getting worse. The bloating hadn't gone down, and was also getting worse. Her tummy was still a little too firm to the touch.

Saf was back on to the GP. This time the possible culprit was colic.

Colic. Great. We'd heard about colic. Everybody's heard about colic. Lots of kids get colic. Must be colic.

But the colic medicine we were told to buy did nothing.

We went online, googling the symptoms. Still none the wiser.

Then one morning, Saf was changing Azaylia when she noticed spots of blood in her nappy. There was another phone consultation. The GP was able to shed no light on it but asked us to monitor the situation.

Next, Saf spotted white spots on Azaylia's tongue. This was thrush, she was told, in yet another phone consultation. Soon she had some medicine for the thrush on her tongue, to add to the medicine she had for her colic, the laxatives, a nasal spray we'd been given for the congestion, and the bulb syringe.

Not long after, Saf and I both had work meetings in Manchester, so we decided to travel together and leave Azaylia with Saf's mum for the day. That morning, just before we left,

Saf had seen a little raised bruise on Azaylia's skin, as well as some weird mottling, and she'd duly emailed pictures over to our GP.

Her mum arrived, told us not to worry, and we left for Manchester. We were both concerned about leaving Azaylia, especially when she was unwell, but we told ourselves it was just baby stuff, and that Azaylia would be okay. Babies are tough, right? And besides, we were going to have to leave her sooner or later. We were working parents, after all.

We were in the car on the way to Manchester when it happened. Saf's phone rang and it was the GP surgery, who having taken a look at the pictures she'd sent that morning, wanted us to get Azaylia to A&E right away. Why? They wouldn't say. Just best to get her looked at right away.

Fear rising, Saf made a call home to tell her mum, 'You need to get Azaylia to hospital,' only to discover that her mum was already in an ambulance on the way to Walsgrave in Coventry. She'd got worried about Azaylia's congestion and, completely independently of the GP situation, called 111 and described the symptoms.

The 111 service had despatched an ambulance.

Whatever was wrong, it was bad.

By now, we had swung the car around and were on our way to the hospital, both of us feeling as though the world had taken a sudden and sickening lurch to one side. The worry we'd been feeling, where we'd told ourselves and each other that we were just being paranoid, panicky parents, it wasn't needless worry. It was real. But even so, if you ask me now what I feared at the time, the answer is that I really didn't know. All I understood was that whatever was wrong with our daughter, it was serious. It had to be. Otherwise they wouldn't have sent an ambulance. An ambulance meant emergency. It meant they were concerned for her life.

As we drove, Saf's mum rang back, and what she had to tell us was that Azaylia's white blood cell count was over fifty. She had no more idea what that meant than we did. Only that it was very, very high. It would have been high for an adult. Azaylia was just eight weeks old.

It's as though something within you plummets. All of a sudden you've gone from, *I'm concerned,* and then *I'm really concerned, I'm getting really fucking worried now,* to having a numb, gut-wrenching feeling in your stomach.

We spoke to Saf's mum again as we reached the hospital, parked the car and dashed across the car park to the main entrance. Azaylia's white blood cell count had risen. It was now at 200.

Still we had no idea what was wrong, other than it was something do with blood cells. Even as terrified as I was, I didn't suspect leukaemia. At that stage I didn't even know about childhood cancer. I thought cancer was something only adults had. You see a statistic on the TV and you think they're talking about grown-ups. Not children. Not babies. Six-week-old babies.

We burst in, virtually crying with fear. *Where is she? Where is she?*

She's having blood tests, they said.

And you know what it's like in hospital. Perhaps you don't. Perhaps you've been lucky enough to avoid that particular experience. Thanks to a list of injuries as long as your arm, I was already a veteran, and what I knew was that things in hospital take time. You wait for tests, and then you wait for the results of those tests. You ask people what's happening, and they don't know. They tell you to wait. And you wait. And you get acquainted with the nearest coffee machine.

Not this time.

Not with Azaylia.

We arrived to discover that she'd been installed in her own room and was being attended to by what looked like a small army of doctors and nurses, and they were already taking blood.

Jostled by busy nurses who in their Covid PPA looked like something from a terrifying sci-fi film, we tried to reach her. All we had was a glimpse of her as they tried to take a blood sample, but I'll never forget the sound she made, squealing as they pricked her toes and her fingers. They were sticking it into her. The thing. Whatever it is they use to take blood. They were sticking it into her but for some reason couldn't get blood so they were pinching her skin and she was squealing, and I stood there feeling stupid and useless and angry and as though I wanted to scoop her up and take her to safety, take her back to our bedroom with a cot beside the bed, away from all these nasty people.

They got the blood. At last she stopped squealing, and we waited.

Except I think it was the same with the results, and that in fact there was no waiting. If I'm hazy on details then you'll have to excuse me, because my head was gone at the time and, honestly, my head goes trying to think about it now. What I do remember is that we didn't have to wait long. I remember, also, that we were in a room and being well-attended to. Not like the situation I just described, where you're having to ask what's happening. There were nurses in and out, checking on Azaylia. This was like no hospital experience I'd ever had before, where a kind of weary tedium is the overall feeling. This was much more urgent than that.

But then it was as though a signal was given and the nurses walked out to be replaced by doctors. Not one doctor, a whole team of them.

I was sitting down as they came into the room.

Muddled and jumbled as my memories are, I remember that very clearly. I remember that I was sitting down.

Because you know how it is when you're about to be given news. You're looking at ways to somehow pre-empt that news. Just to take a few seconds off the wait.

I said to myself, 'Ash, stand up, stand up. Because if you are standing and they tell you to sit down then you'll know something is terribly, terribly wrong.' So I did.

The doctor looked at me. 'We think you should take a seat,' he said.

CHAPTER 29

Leukaemia is the most common type of cancer in children. It's a blood cancer. A cancer of blood and bone marrow during which the body produces an excess of white blood cells. There are two types: acute or chronic. Chronic leukaemia grows quite slowly. Acute leukaemia, well, that grows quickly and without remorse, and in the absence of immediate treatment, the patient will die probably within weeks of diagnosis.

Azaylia had acute leukaemia.

That's what they told me. That's what they told me after I had done as they asked and taken a seat. They told us that Azaylia had leukaemia.

I felt my body go numb. Even now, just thinking about it, it feels the same way. It feels as though my mind is disconnecting from my body.

But that wasn't all. The doctors were telling us that because there are two types of white blood cells, there are two types of leukaemia. First of all, there is ALL, which stands for Acute Lymphoblastic Leukaemia. ALL is the most common type of cancer in children. About 440 kids per year are diagnosed with it, and it's so-called because it starts from the lymphocytes, which are one type of white blood cells, in the bone marrow. It's the most curable form of leukaemia.

The other type of leukaemia is Acute Myeloid Leukaemia (AML), which affects the second subset of white blood cells, the granulocytes or monocytes, both of which come from the myeloid stem cells.

AML is not that common in children. It also has a lower survival rate.

Azaylia had AML.

As they spoke, it was as though each successive word out of their mouths sent me into a worse place. I kept expecting the good news, the note of hope of optimism, but none came; instead it was ... *cancer*. The worst type of cancer. The worst type of the worst type of cancer. And I crumbled. That numbness turned into a complete inability to function. I had no strength in my legs, in my body. I couldn't see or hear properly. I couldn't even stand.

Saf rose to the occasion. Thank God. Even as I tried to get a handle on myself and on the situation, she was rushing to Azaylia's side. Going to her baby.

Her baby who had just been diagnosed with low-survival-rate leukaemia.

But of course they hadn't finished, the doctors. Azaylia would have to be taken to Birmingham Children's Hospital immediately in order to start a course of chemotherapy. The chemotherapy might help extend her life. It *might*. Either way, without it she would probably pass away within a fortnight. We would know more when we reached the children's cancer ward at Birmingham.

And still my mind was separate from my body. Just a few hours ago I'd been like Tigger, bouncing around in a bright cartoon world celebrating fatherhood, giddy with excitement for the life ahead of me. Now it was as though somebody had flicked off the lights and turned everything back to dark. I vividly remember thinking, *I'm going to wake up tomorrow and this is all going to be a nightmare. All a bad dream.*

We transferred to Birmingham. By now it was dark and we were ushered into what was due to be a temporary room, which measured roughly ten by eight foot. In there was a cot for Azaylia and a chair, and that was it. That was where we spent the night. Saf was in the chair, while I lay on the floor, and we listened to our little girl's laboured breathing, and we cried, both feeling hopeless and helpless.

No doubt Saf was thinking the same as me, trying to reconcile the word 'leukaemia' with our life as it was. Thinking back to just hours before when we'd been at home and happy, back to a world that felt like a luxury of security and safety, where we knew that things were going to be all right.

Which had turned out to be an illusion.

They wanted to run more tests, do more observations. Meanwhile, as the next day dawned, we were told Azaylia would need to have a central line fitted. I had no idea what a central line was. I thought it was something to do with the London Underground, but in fact it's an IV tube that goes directly into the patient's chest. It's used to deliver medicine, give blood, and add nutrients, and in order to fit it, they'd need to give Azaylia general anaesthetic. It was a fairly major operation just to insert this thing.

That does your head in, too. The major operation isn't the final step, after which we could mop our foreheads and attend to the business of Azaylia's recovery. It was the *first* step. An operation that would not only need to happen quickly but would be followed by immediate admittance to the PICU, which was the paediatric intensive care unit, a kind of high-level intensive-care-within-intensive-care area where they put the touch-and-go cases.

And with her white blood cell count and temperature spiking, Azaylia went into that category. What she had was not colic or constipation. What she had was hours away from snatching her life away from her.

The operation to fit the central line took place. Saf and I clung to each other like two orphans sheltering in a storm. Next, Azaylia was moved to intensive care. I can't remember whether we were told at the time or if we found out later, but at this point she was critically, *critically* ill, the hospital staff dubious as to whether she'd even make it through the night, let alone through the next couple of days.

Still in the clothes we'd been wearing for Manchester, Saf and I grabbed food and drink from the hospital canteen. Meanwhile, the cruel and awful fact was that the diagnosis had somehow set the cancer free, for overnight it had affected Azaylia's appearance. Her face was now swollen, her eyes puffy. As well as the new central line tube, she now had wires attached to her so that machines could monitor her heart rate, breathing and blood pressure. At first the sound of the apparatus was annoying and intrusive, but like distant traffic noise or a passing train you soon zoned it out.

It was if the bleeping stopped that you'd notice. That's when you'd worry.

CHAPTER 30

The PICU room was so full of machines that there was no room for anything else. No chairs, nothing. Just a small Perspex cot for Azaylia, who looked tiny within it, and the machines themselves.

Somehow, Saf and I found some space in that room. She was in one corner, sitting with her back against the wall if I remember rightly, while I found a sliver of space along another wall, literally a couple of inches wide, where I could lie down but only on my side. The family had mobilised and my brother Ryan had dropped off some yoga mats, so at least we had something between us and the cold hard floor of the hospital.

And that's how we spent our second night in hospital. A Saturday, it was.

It was touch-and-go, that time. Really, *really* touch-and-go. We'd been moved to Birmingham supposedly so that Azaylia could begin treatment, which in this case was chemotherapy, and that the beginning of that treatment would mark the start of her cancer journey. But she was so ill that it had become unlikely she'd even make it through the next couple of days, let alone be able to embark on that journey.

Faced with the uncertainty of what lay ahead, I found my world contracting, my personal walls crowding in on me. There couldn't have been a better metaphor than that tiny cubicle of a room full of machines, and a mum and dad who prayed that a combination of those machines and sheer will would keep their daughter alive. Nothing else mattered right then, and it would be a long, long time before it did.

Thanks to family bringing us stuff, we didn't leave the hospital. Neither of us could think about leaving Azaylia's side. What if something happened when we were away? Even going to the loo was torture.

The staff were great. There was always someone on hand and they were always sympathetic, comforting and understanding. However, the one thing you soon learn in a situation like this is that the doctors and nurses are not in the business of providing false hope. They don't say, 'It's all going to be all right.' They never bring you stories of miracles to give you hope. They don't. They just don't. Those words you really want to hear are never uttered.

'She's going to be all right.'

'This is going to get rid of it.'

'After this, you can go home.'

But the nurses aren't there for that. They're there to do what they do. To do nurse stuff. And there's nobody else you'd rather have doing it. But their job is not to bring hope. If you want hope, you have to look inside yourself.

And that's when something went in me. Saf and I at that point were both in a complete mess. Both floundering, looking to the medics for some glimmer of something and just completely failing to get it. So instead, I said to her, 'Listen, we cannot take our daughter's illness away. We cannot make her better. We cannot change places with her. All we can do is create the most amazing, positive environment around her. And if that's all we can do, then we're gonna do it one hundred per cent.'

We decreed something in that moment: we decided that the room was to be renamed 'Club 100'.

'See that line,' I said, indicating the threshold. 'When you step over this line – and that goes for everybody, everybody who comes into this room – you don't cry, you don't feel sorry for yourself, you don't bring any bad energy inside. You make this room the best, the strongest, happiest, lightest environment it can possibly be. If you need to cry, if you need to vent, if you need to show your negative energy, then you do it elsewhere.'

This was something that we could do. Something that could help … It also formed the beginning of a policy that I've carried with me ever since, and that's the harvesting and nourishing of hope.

Since then, hope has become an essential and fundamental part of my life. Assuming you continue reading, you'll soon understand how hard and deeply that belief would be tested, but for now, I cradled that hope with the same love and tenderness with which I cradled Azaylia. *Hope* that the doctors could do something for her. *Hope* that she wasn't going through too much pain. *Hope* that I could be strong enough for her. *Hope* for a future with our child.

Hope was all we had then. In that room I went from being somebody who wondered what car I wanted to take out that day, which designer clothes I wanted to buy, all that mad, crap stuff, to having literally seven inches in which to sleep.

And that being fine.

That being something I wanted for the next day, and then the next day and then the day after that. Because if I was lying in the same clothes on a cold hospital floor then it meant my daughter was still breathing. She was still alive.

CHAPTER 31

Azaylia was diagnosed with leukaemia on 8 October 2020. On 11 October, still fighting for her life in intensive care, they gave her a little bravery award. The photograph of it is one of my most treasured images of her, and the reason I treasure it so much is because that bravery award really meant something. It meant that Azaylia was fighting. Really fighting.

At the beginning they said she had a day, two days. But then it was getting to day three, day four, day five. She was fighting this thing. Her body was marshalling all the strength within her to do battle against this rare and aggressive form of cancer.

So yeah, it meant something, that award. The pride I felt was off the scale.

Meanwhile, she had become a bit of a little celebrity. A lot of people on the ward knew me through the TV stuff, so they'd come along to the room to see Azaylia, and as soon as they clapped eyes on her, the youngest, smallest, most precious little thing on the ward, well, they fell in love, and from that moment on, she was the rock star. Covid meant they couldn't venture into the room itself, but even so, they could stand and wave to her, and as well as being bowled over by her sheer charisma, they could see how strong and brave she was being.

I was right there with them, marvelling just the same, thinking, *How strong is that little person there? How incredible is that little person?*

And you know what? That strong, incredible little person lived to fight another day. She went from being critical, needing not just intensive but intensive-intensive care, to stabilising. And now, having pulled through that initial, terrifying stage, something happened. Around us we felt as though a little optimism had crept into our lives. Saf and I, the family, even the staff. It wasn't as though anybody was thinking, *She's going to breeze it, she's going to survive*. It was more like, *Phew, we're over the first hurdle.*

Somewhere along the line we were given an update on Azaylia's condition, which was that she had tumours on her lungs, kidneys and in her stomach. We had received this information like punch-drunk boxers, gloves down. *Bang, bang, bang*. Hardly able to process. Just needing to know what could be done now.

Chemotherapy. That was the answer. That was the next step.

A specialist explained the process. Azaylia would begin treatment, during which blue chemotherapy liquid would be pumped into her body for up to thirty minutes twice a day. This would take place over several days, after which she'd have a break for up to three weeks before the cycle would start again.

Each round was therefore a month. Azaylia might only need one round of chemo, said the oncologist, but at that she looked doubtful, as though it would be some kind of miracle. More likely, she'd need up to four.

So they were predicting that we would be in there for at least a month, maybe four. You're allowed to go home for a few days between each block, but mainly that was to be our lives from that moment on. Birmingham Children's Hospital would be our home.

But let me tell you, there was no place we'd rather have been than in that hospital, for reasons I've already said. If we were in the hospital, it meant that Azaylia was still with us, still alive.

Then there was another thing. Chemotherapy treatment is harsh, and that blue chemotherapy liquid is highly toxic. It has to be in order to kill cancer cells as aggressive as the ones lurking in Azaylia's tiny body. For that reason it was possible that she might not survive. The treatment designed to cure her might well kill her.

They put us onto Ward 18, the cancer ward in a brand-new part of the hospital. As regards this new arrangement, it was very much a case of good-news-bad-news. The good news? It was great accommodation. We had a room that was probably two or three times the size of the PICU room, and an ensuite bathroom, TV, the works. It had a big window looking out onto an area lit by therapeutic coloured lights. In terms of hospital facilities, it really was as good as it gets.

The bad-news bit was Covid. During the horrifying time

that Azaylia had been in intensive care, the staff had taken pity on us and allowed Saf and I to stay with her as a couple. Now that she'd stabilised and a treatment plan had been mapped out, one that would keep us in the hospital for the foreseeable future, they needed to abide by the rules more strictly, and that meant only one of us was allowed in the room at any one time.

That was very, very difficult for us to get our heads around. We were saying, 'What on earth are you on about? Only one of us can be here? How is that person going to have support? How is the other person going to cope being away?'

Like, literally, *What are we going to do? How are we going to handle this?*

Then, a stroke of luck. God only knows we needed one. It turned out that if you walked out of the ward, descended the stairs or got in a lift, and left by the nearest exit, then over the road was a Holiday Inn.

Thanks to the foresight and kindness of our family – who among the many other wonderful things they did for us was to have a whip-round – we were able to become permanent residents at the Holiday Inn from that point on. We took a room and devised a system whereby one of us would be on the ward with Azaylia while the other was in the hotel. As the system progressed, it evolved. At first we'd be changing often, like on a twice-hourly basis, but then we developed a more shift-based routine where one of us would stay the night while the other one did the day, and then we'd swap over at midday. We had this system of smooth changeovers. Saf would walk out of the ward just as I'd leave the hotel. She'd take the lift, we'd meet in hospital reception, do a quick review – a status update, if you like – and then go our separate ways.

154

That six- or seven-second handover would have been our only contact every day, were it not for FaceTime. We used it constantly. Saf would fire up FaceTime in Azaylia's room and I would have it on in the hotel room, so that I could chat to Azaylia, talk to Saf, have a little window into the room.

I'd also use it to speak to my mum, auntie and sister. In addition, my mum, who'd barely driven outside of Nuneaton until Azaylia was poorly, would drive to Birmingham every night. She wasn't able to see Azaylia (Covid), and nor was she able to talk to us inside the hotel (Covid). Instead she would stand outside the front window, often for hours at a time, just to chat to us. Other family members came, too. Their concern and support was incredible throughout, but my mum was there I'd say almost every day. She used to ring me in hospital too, to the point where I had to say, 'Mum, I really need to get off the phone now, I'm sorry, I've got things to do.'

During periods between chemo cycles, when my mum could actually *see* Azaylia, she would be at the window of our house, again for ages, often until the early hours, just being there with a cup of tea, watching through the window, occasionally calling, 'Hello, my darling. Hello, Azaylia,' so that afterwards when Azaylia heard my mum's voice, say, just on the phone, she would look to the window, expecting to see Mum there. Incredible. Really incredible.

Nowadays, of course, Mum visits Azaylia's resting place every day, without fail. And she still talks to her.

CHAPTER 32

One of my most vivid memories of that whole time in the hotel was when the family all came together. Keeping to Covid guidelines, they had gathered in the car park, and it became the first occasion that we all saw one another together since the diagnosis. We're a big family, a close family. We hang together and we laugh – God, how we laugh – and everyone's so strong and lively and full of life.

Usually they are.

But not then. Not in the car park of the Holiday Inn, where the hospital buildings cast their shadow; where the family were scattered around, making half-hearted attempts at social distancing, trying to be upbeat and optimistic for my sake and almost getting away with it; almost, but not quite. Mainly looking lost and upset and not knowing what to do with themselves.

But you know what? They were there. They came. Just by

turning up they made me feel so loved and supported, and as I stood there, looking around at their faces, with the realness of the situation crowding in on me, I realised that it was the first time I was seeing everybody properly. I mean really *seeing* them. Seeing them in the sense that nobody had barriers, nobody had a bravado, nobody was being fake. A child dying of cancer does that, I guess. It pierces whatever protective bubble you have around yourself.

That feeling was rare back then. Most of the time it was the opposite, and I'd get a sense of extreme *un*reality every time I was away from Azaylia's room. For me, the realness was inside the ward and inside that room, because in there things boiled down to a matter of life and death, where every hour, every minute, every second was as precious as it was vital. All that Saf and I were focused on was that process of survival, of making sure that Azaylia had the best chance of living to fight another day, that she was as comfortable as she could be in order to fight her fight to the best of her abilities. You could have called me a dickhead. You could have crashed my car. Didn't matter. Everything else but Azaylia was trivial and irrelevant. That was the crucial thing. Her. That to me was real.

The Children's Cancer Ward at Birmingham is light and bright and decorated to be a cheery place, with large colourful murals on the walls. If you were to take away the children, their parents and visitors, you might almost think that it was a place of great joy.

And it can be. There is indeed beauty and joy and so much laughter within those walls. The strength you see on a children's cancer ward will, I promise you, take your breath away.

The fortitude, the refusal to give in and be crushed by the sheer weight of the disease. It'll change your view of human nature. It'll do something to you. Rearrange your DNA.

But there is also great, great sadness. Walking around that ward, I'd see other sick and poorly children. I'd see broken mums and dads. I'd see people who try as they might could not help but be battered into sadness by their struggles. I'd see this and know that I needed to develop a positive mindset for my own poorly child, a state of being that has remained with me to this day. It was why I insisted on Club 100 rules for everyone who stepped over the threshold into our room. It came from a survival mechanism. Me being on a desert island and going, *Okay, how the hell can I survive?* You find two rocks and spark them to make a flame. You find wood and leaves and use them for kindling. You see an animal, kill it, cook it and survive on the fire. You find more wood and start to make a shelter.

Before, if you'd seen two rocks, you'd have kicked them. But in that crucial survival situation, you need every tool, every bit of material. You need skill and imagination to utilise what you find to the best of your ability; you have to make the most of those little things in order to survive.

That's just what I was doing.

It's the same with thoughts, with your mindset. Imagine going into battle, looking at the enemy and thinking they look more fearsome and better-equipped. Your leader doesn't say, 'All right, lads, we're going to lose here.' Because if that's what your leader's saying then you're sunk, aren't you?

No, your leader is the person who has to bring the rest of you up. They have to give you hope, and most of all they have to instil in you the belief that you're going to win. Yeah, you will have negative thoughts that creep into your brain, we all do, but we have to learn to stop them. Me, I take hope and carry it with me like it's a precious jewel. I don't wallow in my misfortune. I nurture a never-say-die attitude. And I don't just pay lip service to this. I genuinely believe it.

But on the other hand, don't get the impression that this makes me an overoptimistic and impressionable guy. I know when the odds don't look good, I know that in order to have positive thoughts you've got to face down the negative ones and, sure, I thought about what might happen. I confronted the possibility of losing Azaylia.

The difference is that I didn't let those thoughts shatter my belief. I was the leader in this situation. Gazing across the battlefield at the enemy I had to believe that we were going to win, and I had to instil that belief in everybody else. No way was I letting thoughts of defeat clamour my brain. Instead I thought, While there's air in her lungs, we're still in the game. While our baby's breathing, we're still in the game. Don't nobody around me be cynical. No cynical thoughts, no cynical words, no cynical actions. From this day onwards we are positive, positive, positive. We create our environment. We create our thoughts. We create our hope and what we believe.

So I took the hit and rose out of the fire. As for Saf, well, it's for her to say exactly how she felt, but I think she'd be the first to admit that she's a bit more glass-half-empty than I am. She would see a reason not to trust somebody rather than the reason to trust them; she would see a reason to fall out rather than want to get on. She might see darkness as opposed to light.

Don't get me wrong, in terms of looking after Azaylia,

she was second to none. But I think she struggled outside the room. When she was with Azaylia, she was the person that she needed to be, and she never faded, failed or defaulted on that. But when she walked out of the room, she walked off a cliff edge; she struggled to get a hold on the gravity of the situation and couldn't find a way through it. And that was where I was able to lift her. I was able to say, 'Come on, Saf, you got this. You got this.'

And it went the other way, too. There were times when she needed to pick me up. For example, there was a weird stage, a period of a week or so, when Azaylia wouldn't respond to me. Normally, I'd be playing with her, lifting her up, singing, dancing, all the stuff I used to do to keep the Club 100 vibe going. But during this particular period, nothing I did had any effect on her. If she was upset and grizzling, she wouldn't calm down for anyone – anyone apart from Saf.

I can't lie. That was a real gut-punch. I didn't know what I was doing wrong. I felt almost rejected by Azaylia. The one thing I could give her was an environment in which she felt safe and loved and as comfortable as possible. Yet suddenly, it wasn't working.

I'm pretty obsessive-compulsive about not giving in. I'll try and try; I'm a real 'if at first you don't succeed' type. But there would come a point when Azaylia just wanted her mother, and at that point it would be, 'You need to come over,' and Saf, however tired she was, would step up and return to the hospital to settle Azaylia.

I wouldn't call her unless it was absolutely necessary, because I'm telling you, those shifts were exhausting. When you got back to the hotel, you'd need your rest. But Saf was never like,

'I've done my time, you've got to sort it out, Ash.' She would be back over before the phone had even cooled down.

And me, I'd slink off, feeling like shit, back to the hotel room, thinking that all I wanted to do was be in the room with Azaylia. Almost as though I was letting the side down.

CHAPTER 33

Even poorly during chemo, Azaylia was always very alert and aware. She really responded to faces and people, and she loved to join in. I used to do a bit of training in the room, shadowboxing and stuff, and she took to clapping along; I'd give her motivational talks in the morning – our 'Let's go, Champ!' slogan came from there – and I swear to God that she hung onto every word.

I loved being with her. I *loved* it. I'm a person who looks for the good and seeks out the silver lining, and some might even say that I do it to an annoying degree, but the fact is that I can't help it. In that situation, I used to think that despite all the terrible shit, the silver lining was that I got to spend so much time with my best friend.

Like, a normal parent is doing other things. You let kids sleep, put on nursery rhymes, whatever. Life goes on. But for those few months in the hospital, my focus was always on her, and because of that, I discovered so much about her. It's how come I knew that singing 'I Wan'na Be Like You' would stop the tears when she was upset; why I felt that I really properly *knew* her as a person, even though she was only ever a baby; why I was so confident that she was a fighter, and that she would have gone on to do great things in life.

Another thing: she was so mobile. Apart from when she was sleeping, she was never still. If she wasn't trying to speak then she'd be wriggling, moving around, trying to grab my beard, swiping at my cap. It was so surprising as her parent and carer to witness. I'd think to myself, *Just lie still, lickle lion, have a rest. Have a rest.*

Azaylia's lion theme became even more pronounced in the hospital. *The Lion King* film she adored, of course, and she loved to snuggle her Nala and Simba teddies. Lions became such an important part of all our lives. You remember that at one stage I wanted to call her Azaylia Lion Cain? That was partly because I always knew she'd have the heart of a lion – and how right I was about that – and partly because we knew she'd be a Leo. But what I didn't know at the time was that the day of her birthday was World Lion Day. Honest to God, look it up if you don't believe me. World Lion Day, 10 August. The day that we celebrate the beauty and power of one of nature's greatest beasts – and in our house, and for me and my family, the day that we celebrate the beauty and strength of Azaylia.

She had various *Lion King* clothes, of course, especially a sleepsuit that was a family favourite. Saf always made sure she looked a million dollars. I mean, we both did, but you have to say that Saf was chief stylist. When Azaylia's hair fell out, she wore pretty little bows and hats. She also had a tiny pair of white mittens she wore to stop her swiping at the tubes.

Ah, yeah, the tubes. As well as the central line, she'd had an NG tube fitted. Short for naso-gastric, this was the tube that went into her nose and was used to feed her if and when she wasn't well enough to drink from a bottle. Saf had begun by breastfeeding Azaylia, but of course those days had rapidly become a thing of the past.

She had other wires attached, and during the time that she was in intensive care we had needed a training session to understand what was going on. Like how the wires were attached to machines that monitored her vital signs – heart rate, breathing and blood pressure – and how they operated on a traffic-light system: green wires were okay to remove for the purposes of, say, washing or changing a nappy. But the red ones, and that included the central line, had to stay permanently in place.

Negotiating the tubes and wires only added to the pressure we felt as her mum and dad. Don't forget that we'd barely gotten used to being new parents as it was. When it came to changing Azaylia, complete with NG tube and central line – and early on in her chemo treatment, a catheter as well – I had to learn a completely new set of skills, thinking, *Okay, I've got to get this baby out of her clothes, change her nappy and wash her, and I've got to do it all without disturbing this line on her chest.*

Same with Azaylia's medication. I felt as though I could almost reach back and touch a time that we were giving Azaylia medicine we'd bought off the shelf in Boots. Now we were giving her something called Oramorph, which I learned is a type of morphine. I had to learn how much to give her and how to flush the line afterwards. Anything that a non-qualified carer could do, I learned how to do.

Saf was always so good at getting stuck in when it came to things like that. I was a bit more apprehensive, but I did it. You think there are all these things you wouldn't be capable of, or that you're not ready for, or that you can't do, but you do them.

And what a learning curve it is.

Imagine this. Picture the scene. You've got doctors explaining the next round of treatment. You've got nurses reminding you to give the medication you have to give every day, three or four times a day, because apart from the chemotherapy, you administer your own medication for your kid. You have to draw it up yourself, get the right measurements, open the lines, administer the medication, flush the lines.

You do all of this constantly. You're mixing things up for feeds. You do the feed and then give her medication, then change her nappy, then wash her, give her another round of medication, and then a change, then a feed. Then the doctors come in and want to talk to you for an hour, and as you're talking, she needs changing, and she's got to be changed right away ...

Why? Why did she need to be changed right away? After all, you can leave a baby for a few minutes, can't you?

Not Azaylia, we couldn't, not only because of worries about the risk of infection, but because the other thing is that, as I said, the blue chemotherapy liquid is highly toxic. To think that we were pumping that awful caustic stuff into our baby was almost too much to bear, but you have to put those thoughts aside and concentrate on the practicalities, like if it went on her skin it could – and indeed did – burn. At first, Azaylia had a catheter fitted but later on that was removed and she'd use a nappy. This blue stuff would come out in the nappy, and if the nappy was left on then it burned.

Which meant that her nappy would need changing immediately. It wasn't like we waited five minutes or so to be polite when a doctor was explaining something. If either Saf or I became aware that Azaylia needed her nappy changing, then her nappy was changed, *that second*. We'd have to wear special gloves to do it, and it became a real race against time: however quick you were – and we were fast – the blue liquid would irritate the skin, and the more chemo she had, the worse her bum became. It got so bad that we were changing her every ten minutes – *literally* every ten minutes.

It wasn't much different if you were on the night shift. Azaylia would need obs throughout the hours of darkness. Hourly, usually, but sometimes every half an hour. You'd be in there and a nurse would bustle in, something bleeping, saying, 'Daddy, nappy.' Of course we were trying to grab a little bit of shuteye if we could, but every half an hour a nurse would appear.

As morning came around, I would have had something like an hour's sleep. A nurse would come in: 'Daddy, she needs her feed,' and so on and so forth.

And you never go, 'I can't, I'm too tired.' You don't do that because in the bed there's a little girl who's battling cancer. Let me tell you, Saf and I used to get so, so tired. Bone-tired. You don't realise until you're suffering from that kind of exhaustion – you don't realise how hard it is to work through it. It's difficult to understand the sheer effort of will needed to move your limbs. Even so, you get up and do whatever needs to be done regardless of how tired you are. You do it because what's the alternative? Turn away?

Was I going to leave the room as Azaylia had acidic blue fluid pumped into her because it was too hard to watch? Or was I going to sit and be there for her? Which kind of man did I want to be? Did I want to be the one who shows up, or the man who turned their back?

When you're presented with the options that we were, you realise that nothing is too hard. It's just a case of are you going to show up or not? Remember that quote from Heraclitus earlier? I urge you to go read it again if you don't. I didn't want to be the guy who shouldn't be there. I didn't want to be a target. I didn't even want to be one of nine. I wanted to be the warrior. The one who brings everyone back.

And that meant being present at every moment, no matter how I was feeling, or how much it hurt. It meant being there no matter what.

CHAPTER 34

Azaylia was always smiling. It may well have been one of the reasons that she so bewitched our followers on social media. She had the NG tube up her nose of course, plasters making sure the tube didn't come out, and yet always on her face was the most beautiful, innocent smile, the smile of a tiny being who knows no bad in the world.

It was a smile that melted the hearts of the world. And the fact that Saf and I were privileged enough to see that smile every day was the greatest honour I can possibly imagine. Some of my most treasured memories with Azaylia were our times on the night shift, when I'd wake up in the chair next to her bed, look over and catch her smiling at me. At times like that I genuinely thought my heart would burst. I thought that no human being can ever possibly love another as much as I love this little girl.

I was lucky – we both were – that although we were in

168

hospital and would rather have been anywhere else, we were still able to see the signs of Azaylia's growth the way 'normal' parents do, and we were able to experience the joy of watching as she developed from a baby to a little person – a person who was learning how to smile, make noises and grab onto things. It was as though Azaylia was determined not to let her disease define her, and I'm sure that at some instinctive level this was absolutely true. She didn't want to 'just' survive, she wanted to thrive. This is what was so amazing about her. It's the reason I talk about how much she taught me. Watching that little girl fight, with hardly even a murmur of complaint, was one of the greatest learning experiences of my life.

Meanwhile, her first round of chemo went to plan. And by going to plan, I mean that it wiped out her illness.

Well, sort of.

In theory.

What actually happens is that chemo sets the body back to zero, including the immune system, which then has to build back up again. The trouble is that as the immune system grows, so the cancer will start to regain its strength. What the chemo does is battle the cancer so that even though it returns, it returns with less vigour than it did in the first place.

The chemo is the killer, though. We were thinking that Azaylia probably wouldn't be able to last the chemotherapy because she was so small and so fragile. And yet, after that first round, she was still there, still fighting. People were coming into the room and commenting on how much she'd grown, how lively she was. You know how I said that she was always so busy, always moving and grabbing and trying to make sounds? Well, she was still like that even after a treatment session. Her little searching eyes would follow you around the room, curious to know what you were up to. Her rosebud lips constantly trying to work themselves around a new sound. Her arms and legs constantly moving. I swear that if we had taken the tube out of her nose then she would have looked just like any other normal baby girl.

At Halloween, Saf and I dressed up, redecorated Azaylia's room in a suitably spooky fashion and then joined in for some Covid-safe trick-or-treating with the other kids.

Thinking about that day reminds me of a time when we were able to bring a little life and light onto the ward. At the same time, I look back at the pictures and see that many of the kids enjoying themselves that day have since died. It's a reminder now, just as it was then, that we were far from the only ones in that position. And it's a reminder that I do what I do with The Azaylia Foundation because she was not the first and, sadly, will not be the last.

I had been sharing our journey on social media, and the papers had picked up on it as well. To be honest, I had gone public with Azaylia's cancer journey practically from the moment of diagnosis. Saf had been opposed to it, but the fact was that I'd been posting about Azaylia since well before she was even born, and continued doing so when she made her entrance into the world. Every time I posted a family snap, or just a cute picture of Azaylia, I'd get hundreds, thousands of comments and replies. Yes, I'd get some of the normal troll-ish crap – that's social media for you – but it was mainly people cooing over how cute Azaylia was.

Then, when things took a horrific turn, we had to decide what to do. Feeling that it was just *too* private, Saf's initial instinct was to shut up shop, and I understood where she was coming from. But my policy was to be open and transparent with supporters and followers; all we had ever done was to be proud of Azaylia, love her and take lovely pictures and lovely videos, and I didn't want that to stop. I also didn't want it to appear as though we were somehow in denial. I'm no psychologist, but I knew enough to know that in order to accept the truth, you need to be transparent about it. But you know what? Mainly I wanted to share the news because she was the one thing on this planet that I was most proud and in awe of, and I wanted to show her off to the world.

We had talked about it for a couple of days and I swear that if Saf had been adamant about not going public then I would have respected her wishes. I think what persuaded her was the fact that we were both finding it exhausting having to keep our family and friends updated. Suddenly we no longer had to explain to casual acquaintances why we'd seemingly dropped off the face of the Earth. We didn't have to go over every aspect of the journey with each individual family member. Instead our family and friends could look at our Instagram accounts and not only be updated on the current situation but be reassured that no matter how bleak it seemed, there was still love and hope in our little family.

So we did. We opened up. And just as it had been when Azaylia was a newborn, seemingly looking ahead to a happy and healthy life, our supporters left messages that encouraged us to continue sharing the details of her journey. And maybe the fact that Azaylia had cancer made it *even more important* that we continued to share the details of that journey.

It all feeds back to that sense of hope, those Club 100 rules.

The trolls would say that we were somehow 'using' Azaylia's illness (to do what, I can't imagine, and they never really said), but I'm confident that we did what we did for the right reasons. And anyway, it wouldn't be long before we were eternally grateful for going public.

If Azaylia was well known in the wider world, that was almost nothing compared to how popular she was in the hospital. There, she was a little star, a magnet for the other kids, their families and visitors. Visitors would have to observe the rules of Covid, of course, but otherwise, all smiles and laughter were welcome in that room – or at least on the threshold. And the one thing they all said was how full of life Azaylia seemed.

Any hope we might have attached to that was misplaced. After that first round of chemo, the doctors were dismayed by how rapidly the disease came back. I had always asked them to tell us the absolute truth. My stipulations were that, firstly, you respect the Club 100 atmosphere, you don't come into this room with your head down, and secondly, that when you come with news, you come with the realness. You are absolutely transparent. You tell us everything.

And what they were telling us was that they didn't think the chemo would work.

They were telling us that it seemed more likely that Azaylia's only hope would be a stem cell transplant.

Okay, we said. Bring it on. Let's do it.

'It's a high-risk procedure,' we were informed. 'She's very small. It will literally wipe out her entire system.'

'What do you mean "wipe out her entire system"?'

'I mean that it can affect a change at a cellular level,' the specialist told us. 'Her eyes could change colour, for example.'

Saf and I looked at each other, both thinking the same. *Her eyes could change ...*

Her eyes. Her beautiful little blue eyes ...

Not that it mattered, of course.

'Her hair could change colour.'

I thought of the soft downy hair on her head.

What we were being told was that Azaylia would still have the mind and thoughts of Azaylia, just she would have somebody else's DNA, and once the operation was complete, she'd have to have regular blood transfusions in order to build up the red blood cells. After the operation it would take at least three months for the new stem cells to make their presence felt, and during this time there was the possibility of something called GvHD, which stands for graft versus host disease. It's when the cells that have been transplanted into the host recognise the host cells as being foreign and attack them.

The other issue was that because of her severely weakened immune system, Azaylia would need to be completely germ-free. This would mean taking our hygiene regime to another level. The way it was put to us, with her immune system so savagely depleted, a speck of dust could kill her. A speck of dust ...

There was another problem, though, of course. There would be no transplant without a donor, and therein lay what was possibly an even bigger mountain to climb.

CHAPTER 35

'We don't have a match for her on the database.'

The problem was one of ethnicity. Azaylia's background was a mix of Caribbean, Burmese, Indian and English. It wasn't just straightforward white-English, black-African, black-Caribbean or Indian.

What I have since learned is that patients from mixed ethnic backgrounds have a 20 per cent chance of finding an unrelated stem cell donor match, compared to 69 per cent of white, European-heritage patients. Something else I discovered was that if we had the funds available, we would be keeping umbilical cords at the point of birth and using them for transplants. But of course we don't, and so we don't.

So that was where we were at: Azaylia needed a stem cell transplant, a high-risk procedure with the possibility of far-reaching side effects. We also needed to find her the right donor, a needle-in-a-haystack process at best.

I guess you could say that this is where I really came into my own. Throughout the process, Saf had kept herself focused on Azaylia. Although we took care of Azaylia fifty-fifty, it was Saf who kept the room organised so that all of Azaylia's gear was exactly where it needed to be. She was the one consumed with the day-to-day detail of caring for Azaylia. I'm not saying that she put her head in the sand, just that our particular skill sets worked that way. She would take the wheel when it came to the fine detail of looking after Azaylia; I'd be the one trying to keep spirits up, trying to instil the right attitude in the room and in our team. Perhaps even more importantly, certainly in this particular scenario, I was also the one to look at the bigger picture. It's just me. Just what I do. That shark-like, have-to-be-moving thing within me.

And now, in the wake of that bombshell, I had something very tangible to do. After talking to the specialist, Saf and I hurriedly agreed that we'd go public. Who knows? One of our followers might be able to help find a donor. Meanwhile, as we went our separate ways, I collared a nurse.

Where do we get the donors from?

Where do you find a match?

What do we do now?

Organisations like Anthony Nolan and DKMS have stem cell registers. It's they who might find a potential donor. Back at the hotel, I went to work. It was mind-boggling how swiftly and horrifically life had changed. We were in the early days of November 2020. Less than a month ago we had been in that warm cocoon of a bedroom in Nuneaton, playing with our little girl and looking forward to Christmas. Now we were in a world of white and red blood cells, platelets, bone marrow and stem cells. A world of 'apparatus', where all the murals and cuddly toys in the world couldn't hide the fact that Ward 18 of Birmingham Hospital was where children died of cancer.

But no, I didn't allow myself to think that way. At least not for any length of time. Giving myself a purpose helped me banish such dark thoughts.

I made my way to the ground floor, out of the door and across the road to the Holiday Inn. We had become friendly with the receptionists, Shelley and Mark. Having already had a bit of a public profile and then documenting our struggles, our story had become one of the most-watched things in the UK, so Shelley and Mark knew the situation and would ask me how we were getting on. As a result we had become friends, although I may have been a bit rude that day, a man on a mission as I stalked through reception and hurried to my room, where I rustled up a contact for Anthony Nolan.

Next. I found a contact for DKMS. And then I made some calls ...

Anthony Nolan is a UK-based charity that specialises in recruiting and assigning donors for what they call hematopoietic stem cell transplantation, which is basically what we were intending to do – in other words, transplant stem cells usually taken from bone marrow, blood, or umbilical cord blood in order that they might reproduce inside the host to produce additional healthy blood cells.

Anthony Nolan work in close proximity to DKMS, which is the Deutsche KnochenMarkSpenderdatei, a more internationally focused organisation with outposts in the US, Chile, Poland, India, South Africa and of course the UK.

While Anthony Nolan recruits donors between the ages of sixteen to thirty and focuses purely on that age range, DKMS will accept donors between the ages of eighteen to fifty-five. Both of them, of course, work with the NHS Blood and Transplant's British bone marrow registry.

All these registries would need to be searched for potential matches. In the meantime my job was to do everything I could to increase the possibility of a successful match appearing. What I was telling both Anthony Nolan and DKMS was that I wanted to use my social media presence to run a campaign for them both. Anthony Nolan, I learned, was – and no doubt still is – desperate for more male donors. DKMS are committed to raising awareness of the need for a constant supply of donors.

Suddenly our decision to 'go public' with the details of our cancer journey seemed like very much the right one. Our plight so far had certainly captured the hearts of the world. Saf's followers on Instagram had increased from around 4,000 to close to a million. I was on almost 1.5 million. We were using other platforms too, plus I had been giving interviews to the press.

I'm not daft – I know the press is a hungry beast. Unlike social media, where a video or cute picture is enough to keep followers interested, the mainstream media like a big story hook, and I had one for them. I was campaigning with Anthony Nolan and DKMS in order to get extra donors.

It was the morning of 4 November 2020, when the doctors told us that chemotherapy was no longer the answer and that a transplant was Azaylia's only hope of survival. By the following day, I had spoken to Anthony Nolan and DKMS and was able to flag up the oncoming campaign. Then, on 6 November, the campaign went live in a post which ran as follows:

Hello to my friends, my family and my followers. As you know, my baby daughter Azaylia has a rare and aggressive form of AML leukaemia that's made even rarer by her being only 8 weeks old when diagnosed. The odds were stacked against Azaylia because they also found tumours in her lungs, stomach and kidneys, which made the doctors uncertain of how well she could cope with the treatment. Despite this, my precious girl has surprised everyone from myself and my partner, our family and even the doctors themselves with how strong she has been and how she has gone above and beyond with battling her illness and dealing with her treatment so far. She couldn't possibly be any stronger and she's doing it all with a smile on her face. Not to say she doesn't have her bad days. 😔🤍

However, doctors have recently informed us that down to the results of her earlier tests that because of the genetic type of leukaemia she has, no matter how well she copes with her chemotherapy and her recovery, the leukaemia will come back, so she now is in desperate need for a bone marrow transplant. As she has an ethnic mix of Caribbean/Indian/White it is much more difficult for her to find a match. That being said, ANYBODY no matter what race could be her genetic match! My little warrior has done all she can do up until this point and more, but now she needs our help! She needs to find a bone marrow donor to give her the fighting chance she needs to potentially beat this terrible illness, ring the bell and return home with us as a family. 🙏 ♡

If this story has touched your heart and my little girl has inspired you, please register as a donor to potentially save her life and maybe thousands of others! 🙏 ♡

All you have to do is fill out a registration form from one of the links provided, do an oral swab test which will be sent to your home and return to the listed address. Something so simple could save my daughter's life! 🙏 ♡

CHAPTER 36

You may well know what I'm talking about when I refer to 'the bell' in that post. It's the bell that chemotherapy patients get to ring when they've come to the end of their treatment. It means your chemotherapy journey is over. It signifies a milestone. It means that all the trauma of that chemotherapy is done.

As well as posts from me and Saf, there was an announcement on the DKMS and Anthony Nolan websites. Beside a photograph of myself, Saf and Azaylia was a story calling for more life-saving stem cell donors. As the story pointed out, we were relying on somebody not known to us who could save Azaylia's life.

It was 6 November 2020, a Friday. That weekend, as the campaign kicked into gear, 80,000 people registered to be stem cell donors. To put this in perspective, it was more than both organisations had had in the last four years, combined. People volunteering to be donors were asked to order a kit and do a swab to see if they might be a match, which in the first instance, would establish whether or not they were a match for Azaylia.

But both Anthony Nolan and DKMS were clear that those coming forward as a result of our campaign had to be aware that they weren't just volunteering for possible inclusion in Azaylia's bank; they would be on the register for the rest of the country, even the rest of the world, to possibly benefit.

And 80,000 of them said, 'Fine. No problem. No worries. Bring it on.'

She did that.

You did that, Azaylia. You did that.

And this was just over the first weekend. Within a week we had 150,000 people coming forward.

It's insane, isn't it? It's insane and mind-boggling and really, really humbling. Everyone who came forward, I thank them from the bottom of my heart. I thank them for not scrolling away when they could so easily have done. I thank them for turning what must have been a good intention or an idle thought into actual reality. I thank them for what they did to help the cause of blood cancer throughout the world.

And you know what? Because of Covid I had hundreds, actually thousands, of messages from people who told me that Azaylia's story helped them survive the pandemic. People who would describe how they sat at home with their Sky TV and their warm bed and friends and drinks, and all of these home comforts, yet still feeling sorry for themselves, and then all of a sudden they would see Azaylia's plight and realise how fortunate they really were.

They become invested in our little girl – invested to the

point where in one weekend, 80,000 of them did something about it, and then in the weeks to come another hundred or so thousand did it too.

That's powerful, man. That's really powerful. In the short time she was in the world, Azaylia gave it many great things. The fact that 200,000 cancer sufferers might have had a shot at a transplant thanks to her is right at the top of her list.

In the meantime, the chemotherapy continued. Our days of shifts and feeding medication and nappy changes resumed. For the second month, however, the chemo plans changed. We were now preparing for a stem cell transplant. This was the 'conditioning treatment' phase of the process, the idea being to destroy any existing cancer cells prior to the procedure and also to shut down the body's immune system and thus make it less likely that the transplant would be rejected.

As the days wore on, we waited for news. I wore orange to represent 'faith over fear', for leukaemia awareness, and publicly pledged to do all I could to devote myself to fighting leukaemia and helping its sufferers.

Meanwhile, we were able to take Azaylia home in between for a few days, having completed her first block of chemotherapy. She was poorly then, but the oncology department had recommended that a dose of home life might be good for both her and us, just to boost our morale and replenish energy reserves before going back for another round.

To say we made the most of our time is putting it mildly. Why? Because if all went well and a donor was found we would return to the hospital for a second block of chemotherapy and then stay there during her stem cell transplant.

In short, we were expecting to be in hospital, not just for Christmas but possibly months afterwards.

Our days at home were just too short. In the end we had three days before we had to go back to the hospital so that the oncology department could do the necessary: replace her NG line and service her central line prior to her second round of chemotherapy.

Still we waited. Azaylia had her chemo. I stayed upbeat and smiling. I sang for her and danced. When allowed, I took her on little trips around the hospital and she loved the nurses making a fuss over her. But it was so difficult to see the damage wrought by the chemo and cancer drugs. They may be aimed at killing cancer, but they kill the good stuff too. Just because she was a baby and unable to articulate her pain didn't mean she was safe from suffering the hair loss, nausea and vomiting, weight loss, bruising, bleeding, breathlessness, sore throat, mouth and stomach, high temperature and open wound sores on her neck and bum.

Still, those smiles that I had imagined when she was a newborn were real smiles now. Even when the effects of her treatment were at their worst, she still never stopped grinning. A beautiful smile, it painted the room in sunlight.

And then we found a donor.

It didn't come as a result of the campaign.

It came from an umbilical cord donor.

This was great news. It meant that the donated stem cells would come from a baby and therefore be effectively 'new'.

'So how did that come about then?' I asked. 'Did the parents register the baby?'

No, I was told. Just that some places do it as a matter of course. They test cords – they keep cords and test them.

One bittersweet aspect of that process was that we would never know the identity of the donor. It's just the way the system works. Had it been a donor who registered via one of the usual avenues, we would have been able to meet and thank them, but when it's a baby donor, you just don't know. You never find out. Typical Azaylia, of course. Nothing ever happened the easy, simple or straightforward way. She gets cancer, she gets a rare, high-risk cancer. She needs intensive care, she goes into intensive-intensive care. The cancer goes and then it comes back even more aggressively and now she needs a stem cell transplant …

'What are the chances of it working?' we ask them. They won't answer.

'As a percentage? Ninety? Seventy? Eighty?'

'We can't say.'

There's a chance. That's all they would say, and that's all we needed, the only bit of driftwood that we as drowning people needed to cling onto. We grabbed it with both hands. We took that hope to our chests. We cradled it like it was made of precious material.

We had a chance. That's all we needed. All we needed in order to carry on with faith, carry on with belief, and carry on being the best people that we could be in order to make Azaylia's time in hospital as happy and fun and as light as it could possibly be.

Just before Christmas, at the same time as ITV News ran a piece about the success of the donor appeal, we were preparing for Azaylia to go back into surgery. She had to have a bone marrow aspiration, which involved what is basically a lumbar puncture – in other words, the insertion of a large needle into her bone in order to extract bone marrow fluid and check it for signs of cancer.

At the same time she was fitted with a second central line so that medics had a choice of infusion points for her medication and chemo. As I say, there was never any easy route with Azaylia.

CHAPTER 37

In order for Azaylia to have the transplant, we had to leave Ward 18, which had been our home for so long.

And when I say 'home', I really mean it. The nurses, the patients and their families were 'the people of the ward' just as we were, and because they were people who we'd seen far more regularly than members of our own family, they had become like family to us. There's no doubt about it, a cancer ward can be a harrowing place. If you walk around, you see cubicles, and though the place is decorated and furnished in as uplifting a way as possible, that won't compensate for the sights you see, which are children, very, very poorly children. Children with tubes and wires sticking in them. Children with no hair, sunken eyes, sallow skin. Children in wheelchairs, gripped by the misery of cancer and the treatment they hoped would save their lives.

Like I say, tough.

Yet, the atmosphere in that place ... Wow, man, it was beautiful. It was really, really beautiful.

We used to leave our door open. You'd have a mum walking along the passageway with her daughter, and I'd hear her little girl say, 'Can we see Azaylia?'

'I'm not sure, sweetheart ...' I'd hear the mum say in response.

But I'd be like, 'Of course you can, darling, of course you can.'

Curse Covid and the rules that stopped them coming into the room (although we were quite rightly terrified of infection and so we always abided by them), but they could wave hello from the doorway, and be asking after her: 'How are you? How are you doing?'

It was a two-way street, too. We'd take gifts to other parents and kids and pay visits to their cubicles just as they paid visits to us. It felt as though we were friends with everyone. I'd be sitting with Azaylia in our room, look across the corridor at the room opposite, where there'd be another parent with their kid, and we'd talk and tell our stories, share our fears and our hopes.

The thing was that as a little baby, Azaylia was the youngest one on the ward. Everybody else was older, going right up to teenagers. That just made Azaylia even more attractive. People loved to see her. They loved to try and make her smile. I'd be doing something silly with her, jumping up and down or pulling funny faces or singing in a funny voice to try and make her laugh, and I'd glance over to the doorway and see somebody there watching me. The amount of times that nurses walked in and caught me making a fool myself, I couldn't even begin to count.

So, yeah. It was a beautiful place, Ward 18. A beautiful

place full of amazing children, amazing parents, and the best nurses in the world.

But then we had to move to Ward 19, the transplant ward, and all of that stopped.

Now things were getting serious. Shit got real, as they say. The room had an area in which you'd have to get changed, take off your outdoor clothes and wear coveralls. It was like going into a high-security jeweller's, where one door closes and then another opens. But the irony with that comparison was that all jewellery was banned. It had to come off. Inside, everything would have to be wiped down. It had to be spotless.

The journey from one to the other was short, a little walk along a corridor. But what was significant about this particular corridor was the fact that along it, fixed low so that a child could reach, was the famous bell.

I couldn't help but look at it on the occasions that I walked past, thinking of the times I'd been sitting in Azaylia's room and heard it ring, accompanied by a round of applause from well-wishers.

That could be us, I always thought.

No.

That *will* be us, one day.

One day soon.

And now, on our way to the transplant ward, as we passed the bell, it felt as though we were one step nearer.

The idea of relocating was to get Azaylia used to the ward and get us accustomed to the protocols of being there, which involved very, very strict adherence to cleanliness. As if we weren't already under the cosh of Covid procedures, with the medical staff all wandering around looking like the evil government guys in *E.T.*, the whole place covered with black and yellow tape, notices everywhere telling us do this, don't do that, now we had an extra level of hygiene to think about.

Even so, and despite the fact that we'd had the importance of cleanliness drummed into us, the room wasn't always as clean as we would have liked. I often wandered around wearing either flip-flops, socks or sometimes I had bare feet. One time I happened to look at the sole of my foot and saw that it was dirty.

I called in a nurse and pointed it out. Now, obviously, the last thing you want to do is increase the workload of a nurse. And the second-to-last thing you want to do is have a nurse *think* that you're about to increase her workload. Nurses start the day with a full plate and that plate only gets fuller as the day wears on. They spend their entire time firefighting. Saf and I were big question-askers; we wanted to know everything there was to know, but we were always acutely aware that while a specialist might take a moment or so to explain something to you in layman's terms, nurses simply didn't have the time. They were great, don't get me wrong. I have nothing but love and respect for all of them, but they're like cruise missiles: you don't want to get in their way. You don't want to try and pull them off course.

And bearing all this in mind, I was super careful to make sure that this wasn't the case. I wasn't getting ratty with this nurse, I was just wondering if there were cleaning products available so that Saf and I could clean the room ourselves.

No, I was told. The cleaner comes in. They use special stuff blah, blah, blah. But even with all the PPA and the hygiene protocols, staff are still wandering in wearing the same Crocs and Skechers that have been elsewhere in the hospital. Nobody could help that.

And so, as we had done throughout the entire process, we took matters into our own hands. Together, Saf and I became absolutely fanatical about keeping the place clean. I mean, we were told that the room had to be spotless, and if the hospital weren't going to abide by their own rules, then we would do it for them.

We used the Clinell sterilised wipes to scrub the floors, the walls and the apparatus. Our policy of changing Azaylia straight away continued; the practice of constantly washing our hands not only continued but increased, to the extent that my hands had started to crack and bleed.

Meanwhile, our clothes would be washed at a high temperature, tumble-dried and given back to us in sealed bags. The idea was that they wouldn't leave the hospital and that all we'd have to do was keep ourselves showered. Clothes were the last thing on my mind, so the way I played it was to buy four baggy tops, four baggy pairs of shorts, four pairs of boxers and socks and just wear them all of the time.

Just as an aside, I remember that on one of our rare visits back home, I walked into the room in which I kept all my clothes. They were such vivid reminders of another life, a life before all this. Would you say I'd come a long way since the old party-loving, reality TV star? I was still working out. Fitness had become a vital means of keeping my head straight within all of the hospital madness. But otherwise? The tenacity was there. The will. The fire. But those qualities had been reshaped and reframed. They were now directed towards the fight to keep Azaylia alive. I knew now that all material concerns were trivial and irrelevant. Everything was trivial and irrelevant – everything – compared to matters of life and death.

And later, I would end up giving those clothes away. Somebody else needed them more than me.

But anyway, back to Ward 19, and all the new regulations around cleanliness. You'd have thought we had enough to deal with, but guess what?

It was great.

Yes, I missed the familiar friendly atmosphere of Ward 18, where I was among my people. But life on Ward 19 was next level and next level meant the next step in the journey. Everything has to be right for this procedure.

Things were so very different on Ward 19. Not just the cleaning thing. Nobody wanders around the transplant ward. You don't hang around making small talk in the doorways of other cubicles. There's no distant sound of music or laughter, and there aren't many murals or cuddly toys either. It's a place of great industry and purpose.And that purpose is to perform the procedures that keep people alive.

For a fortnight or so we waited for the results of the bone marrow procedure. During this time came New Year's Eve – Christmas having passed in a blur – and we were allowed to go home, which is where we were when we got the call to return to hospital.

It was time – it was time for Azaylia's transplant. With our usual battle cries of, 'Let's go, Champ,' we chucked all our stuff in the car and gladly returned to the Holiday Inn and Birmingham Hospital.

But.

There was a problem.

Of course there was a problem. According to the results of the bone marrow aspiration, Azaylia had relapsed after her second round of chemo. If we needed proof just how aggressive was her form of leukaemia, then here it was.

And that was just the beginning of the bad news. The fact that she had relapsed meant that she would go into her transplant with leukaemia, which was far from ideal. It put her in the high-risk category for complications and the poorest category for success.

Would the transplant still go ahead? Yes, but grim-faced specialists were telling us that this kind of procedure on a baby of Azaylia's size was a risk, a big risk – especially with a cancer as aggressive as hers.

The transplant, we were told, would wipe out her neutrophils, which are the type of white blood cells that support the immune system and help the body fight infection. This was a complete reboot. Again we were told that we were effectively taking somebody else's DNA, possibly changing Azaylia's blood type, as well as the characteristics she had been born with. Again it was stressed that any kind of infection would be life-threatening. Again we were explained the risks of GvHD.

In short, the operation could go horribly wrong. But …

And this was what we were clinging to. This was my whole creed.

It could reduce the strength of the cancer so that more rounds of treatment would kill it. It could even get rid of the cancer altogether.

CHAPTER 38

With everything that had happened, and with all the talk about how high-risk the stem cell transplant would be, it's fair to say that I had pictured something different when it came to the operation itself.

What was I expecting? I'll tell you. A huge room. Lasers. Artificial arms. Ten doctors with ten nurses wiping their brows as they worked desperately against the clock. You know the drill ...

But no. None of that. Instead the procedure took place in Azaylia's room on the ward. The only slightly science-fiction aspect to it was a drum which, when opened, let out a billow of what looked like dry ice, but was probably something way more sophisticated than that, and from it extracted the all-important donor material, all of it done in conditions of absolute sterility. After that they simply attached a really big syringe to her central line and flushed her system with the new material.

The whole process took – what? – ten minutes?

The way that Saf and I played it was that we took it in turns to watch half the procedure each. She had been in there from the night before, did a few minutes of the transplant then rang me, and I ran up to be there for the second part of it. According to Saf, the room had filled with the smell of sweetcorn when the drum was opened.

So that was it. Just a big injection really. If I was being flippant, I'd say that we probably could have done it ourselves.

But I'm not being flippant, not when it's about my daughter's stem cell transplant. Besides which, the risky stuff comes in the immediate aftermath when virtually the whole department is on high alert, waiting to find out how the patient will react.

The host could, for example, have an instant reaction to the new stem cells and reject them straight away – in a matter of moments.

Thankfully, that didn't happen. Now, then, came the waiting game. It was a case of keeping everything crossed and wood permanently touched to see whether the operation would work, and if so, what percentage of engraftment we might have. 'Engraftment' is what happens when the new stem cells make their way to the bone marrow and begin to produce healthy white and red blood cells. According to the specialists, it could take months. There was talk of a transplant in that very hospital where the engraftment process had taken a year. The more likely prediction was that it would take months. Obviously the ideal outcome was that Azaylia would have 100 per cent engraftment but as usual with the medics, they try and manage your expectations. Not everyone will reach that, we were told.

In the week or so after the transplant, Azaylia really didn't look well. Just as she had throughout the entire process, she experienced side effects. She had something called mucositis, which is an inflammation of the mouth, as well as sickness, skin dryness and constipation. Saf and I were cleaning her almost constantly, applying the wipes we been given – Conti wipes, a type more delicate than the standard – with even more care than usual, which, let me tell you, was already a lot of care.

This tiny, precious thing. That's what I used to call her so much. 'You're so precious,' I would say to her. We treated her as though she were made of the world's most delicate and breakable substance. She was on so much medication: drugs for anti-sickness, post-op anti-rejection drugs, medication to help support her liver, other medicines designed to relieve the side effects. God only knows what was going on in that little body.

Then, of course, was the fact that she'd gone into the procedure still with leukaemia, and what this meant was that even as she recovered from the operation and during the engraftment period, she would need more chemo.

And yet, at the same time, we marvelled at how strong and robust she was. She'd wake up some days looking really, really ill, and yet the smile remained and she never failed to respond to some of my little tricks – the jumping-up peekaboo game, for example, always made her giggle. And did I imagine it, or did she respond to the sound of my common mantras: 'You got this,' and of course, 'Let's go, Champ.' Did I imagine it or did she really perk up at the mention of her nickname, 'lickle lion'? Either way, that fighting spirit never flickered, never faltered. Even when the tears came, we felt like it was still there.

We wished she could communicate though. God, how we

wished that. I think that our situation was practically unique, perhaps throughout the whole hospital, in that Azaylia was never able to tell us how she was feeling. It was one of the most heart-breaking aspects of the whole process. Thinking back to the time before the diagnosis, we used to wonder how long she'd been in pain before we raised the alarm, and how severe that pain had been.

I tried to reassure Saf, but I know she felt guilty about that, as did I. We'd been fiddling about with colic and thrush medicine, laxatives and nasal syringes when all the time the real threat had been so much worse.

So just as Azaylia was unable to tell us of her suffering, so she was unable to tell us whether or not she was feeling better. What we had was just her facial expressions, her general demeanour, and we hardly dared think it. We hardly dared admit it to ourselves, let alone to each other but …

Was she looking better?

Certainly the medical staff seemed to think so. Often from them we would hear things like, 'Your daughter is strong.' 'Your daughter is amazing.' Oncologists, doctors, nurses … We allowed ourselves to believe. We reminded ourselves that when it came to beating the odds, Azaylia was a veteran. She'd been doing it since the beginning of her journey and she was doing it now.

Our hopes were raised even more when, at the beginning of February 2021, the consultants told us that they would be weaning Azaylia off her medication on the basis of her incredible progress. That also meant that there were extended periods when she was no longer hooked up to her central lines, and so we could at last pick her up and play with her.

Meanwhile, I had shaved my hair off in sympathy, so that Azaylia and Daddy could be the same, and I did so thinking about the concept of heroes. How when you're young, your heroes are footballers, and if David Beckham gets a new haircut, you want to follow suit. If Cristiano Ronaldo has a new pair of boots, you're lusting after those boots. I was no different. As a kid, and then really as a young adult and into manhood, I was always worried about the way I looked and what people thought of me.

But now I gazed upon my daughter and I realised that I didn't care about any of that stuff. I didn't care what I was wearing, as long as I was close to her. I didn't care how I felt, as long as she was okay.

And I looked at her and I thought, *Who's my hero? You are.*

So I got some clippers and in my hotel room, I shaved off my hair. As I did so, I thought of her. I thought, *I want to be like you. I want to look like you.* I thought of the other kids who don't have the luxury of deciding whether or not to keep their hair. Like I'd often hear from other parents how the kids felt so self-conscious without hair, the girls especially. 'Oh, she's lost all her confidence,' I'd hear. And yet the bravery, the strength …

Not only did I want to stand in solidarity with them, but it went further than that. They were my heroes. They were the people I wanted to emulate.

I was nervous when, having completed the big shave-off, I entered Azaylia's room. What if she didn't recognise me? But she did, that famous smile appeared, and as usual the sunshine broke through the clouds and I felt my heart swell.

Azaylia had awakened me to the world. She was bringing

out a side in me that was rarely seen, putting me in touch with my feelings and my emotions. She inspired me. And that, to me, is hero material right there.

For Valentine's Day 2021, Saf put Azaylia in a white vest with 'Azaylia loves Daddy' printed across the front. Those two know how to make a grown man cry.

You'd have to say that things were really looking up now. There was an air of expectation and optimism around us. The nurses were diligently informing us of routines around Azaylia's care and medication. Why? Because the way it was going, it looked like we would soon be discharged.

No doubt about it we had a good feeling. Throughout the process I had always worked hard to maintain a positive energy, but all of a sudden it felt like I didn't need to work as hard as usual. That positive vibe was already there, already present.

And so when we were called into a meeting with the specialist, we went with hope in our hearts. Despite a life-time of injuries and setbacks and sometimes just plain terrible luck, a life in which the cruel hand of fate seemed to have played too much of a greater part than usual, I went into that meeting with optimism.

CHAPTER 39

A nd for once that optimism was repaid.

'Your daughter is very strong,' we were told, before being given the news that Azaylia had engrafted. Not in a year or four months, but five weeks. She had fully engrafted and done so with 100 per cent success. There was no GvHD, no infection, nothing.

The transplant had been a success.

The feeling was like a tidal wave of relief and happiness, and there's no other word for it, pure *joy,* that swept through me, and through Saf too. It was like somebody had pulled a plug within me and from it poured black tar and into it came sunlight. Like an unseen force standing with giant hands on my shoulders suddenly let go. It was, without doubt, the best feeling in the world. Getting a pro football contract, getting accepted on some TV show, things that at the time I thought were amazing, life-changing events. They were nothing – absolutely fucking *nothing* – compared to this.

'That's it,' I was yelling, already out of my seat. 'She's a champ! I knew she could do it.'

A rare smile from the specialist.

There was of course a 'but'. As we knew by now, you always get a 'but'.

She would remain under observation on Ward 19. She would need a bone marrow aspiration just to check that the operation has been a success, as thought. She would still have to be monitored in case the cancer returned. But otherwise? We'd anticipated having to stay on Ward 19 for months and months, maybe even up to a year. But now, Azaylia, at six months old, having been in hospital since she was eight weeks, was finally going to come home for good.

On the morning of 18 February, she went into surgery for her latest bone marrow test. We were told that we'd have to wait a fortnight to know if she was clear. In other words, whether the transplant had been as 100 per cent successful as we were told.

To be honest, this was one of those times when I was in opposition to the medical professionals. Don't get me wrong, they're experienced doctors and I'm an ex-footballer and reality TV star, but I was also Azaylia's daddy; I'd been with her every step of the way throughout her leukaemia journey, and I knew a thing or two about her disease. I knew that it was ruthless and, most of all, that it was fast.

'Why wait?' I was saying. 'Why wait so long to get the lumbar puncture? It's not going to take a month to trickle back, it's going to come back with a vengeance, do you know what I mean?'

No, I was told. Leave it to us. Or words to that effect.

In the meantime, we were advised to begin preparing for a life outside of the hospital and Holiday Inn. Goodbye, Shelley and Mark, we were going home. Azaylia would still be under the care of the hospital and would need to return for blood tests and other appointments, but she would no longer be a permanent resident. At that very moment in time, there was no better word in the world than 'outpatient'.

Now, at last, we were making plans for a future as a family. It would not be without its hardships, of course. You don't just shake off leukaemia like you shake off a cold. For a start, there were all the tests you need, the medication and around-the-clock care. Plus, of course there was the ever-present risk of infection. Saf set about giving our house the clean of its life. For God knows how long, she was a blizzard of Clinell wipes until the house was not just spotlessly clean – it always was anyway – but an almost completely sterile environment.

An environment safe for a poorly little princess.

She came home, and you can imagine the scene. I mean it was a Covid-safe scene, a scene appropriate for a baby in remission from cancer, but still something of a scene. There were of course appointments to keep, and we were back and forth from the hospital, but at home we were a family again. Mummy and Daddy in their bedroom, Azaylia in a crib by the side of the bed, or in the bed with us, and every morning I woke up and I thanked the good Lord for delivering us from the hands of cancer. Back before Azaylia's diagnosis I used to talk about how she was going to be a tennis player when she grew up. We'd be talking about how she could go to university, but also that we wouldn't pressure her into doing anything she didn't want to do; that she should always choose her own path in life.

I'll be honest, I never really stopped doing that, even when she was in hospital. But I'll be even more honest and say that sometimes I wondered if my words had a hollow ring. After all, it's one thing being upbeat, quite another to tempt fate.

Now, though, I felt as though I was talking about the future with confidence. I was talking about a future I felt sure existed.

'Soon,' we told her, 'soon we will be ringing the bell.'

Until that day came, 23 February it was. Bubbling over with excitement, we clambered into the car, made our way back to the hospital.

This was the day that Azaylia would finally ring the bell.

CHAPTER 40

We arrived at the hospital where Azaylia was due for some blood tests. And then to ring the bell. Nurses had lined the corridor, a guard of honour along the passageway between Wards 18 and 19, and we were on the verge of the big moment – a moment that we had hoped, prayed and dreamed of for what felt like so long – when our oncologist asked us to step to one side.

There were tears in her eyes.

Now, our medical team, humane as they were, rarely betrayed any emotion.

So that was bad. That was the world lurching again. That awful sea-sick feeling.

'I'm sorry …' she began. She closed her eyes as if to summon the strength for what she had to say next. 'Azaylia has relapsed.'

The feeling was like being punched in the head, like running blindfold into a brick wall. You've heard the expression 'stunned silence'. For a moment or so neither I nor Saf could summon the words, until one of us said, 'But ... we won. You told us that we won. All the tests ...'

The tests. Exactly. They had all confirmed that Azaylia was cancer-free. All the tests except for one, the one that we had thought was a formality, the most recent bone marrow test.

We had been told that the results would take a fortnight to appear, but in fact they had come early.

'I'm sorry, she's relapsed.'

'No, no. She ... Sorry, say it again.'

'She has relapsed and it's bad. Not only has the disease returned, but we found more tumours. We found tumours in her lungs, in her stomach, in her liver, in her kidney, in her spleen. In everything.'

Another punch in the head. Another punch in the head. Another ...

All of the strength I had summoned, all that positivity and hope. It was as though it all drained out of me. Temporarily, as it was to turn out, and for that I'm very thankful, but as I stood there with Saf and we heard the news the white light flicked out, and the thick black tar returned. My whole body felt heavy.

And here's the thing. Here's what made it even worse if you can imagine such a thing. Normally when you speak to the experts, they give you the news, bad news normally, and then right away outline what happens next.

Not on this occasion. This time it was, *Azaylia's relapsed. We don't know what to do.*

In other words, they were out of options.

What that meant was ...

No, they didn't need to tell us what it meant.

We knew.

Now the tears came. Both of us. Saf and I crying, unable to see a way forward, hardly able to even process the news.

I mean, think about it. We'd had October, November, December, January, February, all that time of constant worry. Then to be told that the battle is over and you've won and then, in the split second before you make your final walk to victory, it's all taken away from you.

Somebody was saying something about ringing the bell being called off, but I found myself, without even thinking about it really, saying, 'No, let's ring the bell. She deserves to ring the bell. Everybody's waiting. She deserves it.'

Carrying Azaylia, we made our way along the corridor to the bell, where the guard of honour still awaited our arrival. I looked at their faces and could see that, like us, the nurses and staff were hiding their tears and burying their true feelings. We did it for each other's sake, of course, but mainly we were doing it for the sake of that little girl. That little girl who had been through so much …

And deserved to ring her bell.

We went through the motions, shellshocked and hollow, and we made the right noises when the sound of the bell shocked Azaylia and made her cry.

She was presented with a certificate, and in a voice trembling with emotion, I said a few words, thanking the nurses for all their care, acknowledging that the cancer had returned, 'but that just means that we stay positive like we have all the way through, and we get back to fighting so we can ring that second bell.'

And then we retreated back up the corridor, grateful for the Covid masks that hid our faces and kept our true feelings from spilling out.

We returned for part two of the meeting. The one where, surely, they would outline a treatment plan, tell us what to do next.

No. There was no treatment plan. The treatment plan was there was no treatment plan. They wanted to send Azaylia home. They wanted to send her home for end-of-life care.

'We're not doing it,' I told them. 'We're not taking her home to die.'

CHAPTER 41

Whatever people say, I like to think that patience is one of my strengths. Most days, I'm pretty patient. But where my patience wears thin is hearing people with opinions which betray the fact that they have no perspective. You got a dent in your car. So fucking what. It's just a dent. It's just a car. Is it life or death? No? Then, honestly, shut up about it.

My life's been a rollercoaster. It's been rocked and rocked and, quite honestly, there are times when I feel totally maxed out by it.

And that was one of those times.

'Get the whole team in here,' I said. 'I want to see everyone now. Oncologists, specialists, everyone.'

I often say that the story of Azaylia and I is a tale of *Beauty and the Beast*. The Beast is gentle, right? He's a romantic soul. But he's got teeth. He will protect what he loves. I don't suppose that the medical staff had seen that Beast side of me. Not until that moment – not until they were all assembled.

'I'm going to tell you something,' I began. 'You guys might see poorly children every day, but this is my poorly child, and I'd die for that child. I'd do anything I can to stop my poorly child having to leave this Earth. That's what you need to understand. I am a vicious and protective and caring and loving father, and I'll do what it takes to keep my baby here for as long as possible. That's what you need to know about me.

'You say you have no options for Azaylia, but believe me, you do. And if you really think you don't, then you'd better find some, because if we have a one per cent chance, just a one per cent chance, then I'm gonna take it, and you are gonna give it to us. For you, this is a decision based on whether the treatment will cure her or not.' I shook my head. 'But not for us. For us, every single minute of every single day that we spend with our baby is precious and as long as she's still smiling, as long as she's happy, then I don't care whether it's a cure, whether it's maintenance, whether it gives us a glimpse of hope for a chance, but we are *not giving up*.' I glared at them. 'You understand what I'm saying? Because if you think that we're giving up and going home, then we have a problem on our hands.'

That was it. I'd set my stall out.

And if there's anyone out there who thinks I was being unfair on the overworked medical staff, then yeah, I get it. I understand where you might be coming from. I express myself with passion, and I'd never deny that.

But don't forget that you weren't there. I was. I'd been in the system now for all those months, twenty-four hours a day.

I knew how they operated. I knew that when they tell you they can't, they can. I knew that when they tell you they won't, they will.

Threatening? No. Serious? Abso-fucking-lutely.

So what I did was set out the rules of the game. I told them, *This is what we're going to do, people. Better get used to it.*

They may have been shocked. They may have thought that a mask had slipped. But they would have been wrong about that. It wasn't that a real, more belligerent version of me suddenly made its presence felt. It was a question of one thing and one thing only: it was a question of survival.

I'm not saying that the specialists were letting us down, by the way. It wasn't as though they were restricted by red tape or hampered by budgetary considerations. They just didn't know what to do or where to turn next. They couldn't see a way through the darkness. I was saying, 'Buy a torch.'

We went home. It was agreed that Azaylia would stay an outpatient and also that we should reduce her cyclosporine medication as there was a chance that the absence of the medicine, which was helping to regulate her new stem cells, would in fact give them a boost and help them to fight the cancer cells.

Following that particular role of the dice, she would have yet another bone marrow aspiration, after which we'd have to wait two weeks to find out whether or not the cancer was in retreat or not. Chemo, we were told, was no longer an option. If she still had leukaemia after the next bone marrow test, then ...

It wasn't something we wanted to contemplate. Instead, we enjoyed our time at home with Azaylia, returning to hospital twice a week for bloods. It was during this period – on one of our visits to hospital, in fact – that Azaylia spoke what may well have been her first word.

I was in her room with her, on FaceTime with my mum and my sister, who were recording me playing with her. All of a sudden there it was: 'Dadda.' Probably her first word, and what a hit it was. What an honour. I felt almost blessed by it, as though the word came not from her but from some higher being.

On 23 March, the day after Mother's Day, and exactly a month after we had rung the bell, we packed our stuff and left for what would be Azaylia's final bone marrow test. Yet again she would need to go under anaesthetic – Saf and I both agreed that we *hated* her being sedated – and with so much riding on the outcome, we could hardly bear to think of it.

The bone marrow tests came back. The leukaemia was still there. The transplant had to all intents and purposes been a success, but it didn't matter. The leukaemia had returned. We had hoped that the last throw of the dice might work.

It was not to be.

So was that it? Were we giving up?

No.

CHAPTER 42

At some point, a woman on social media called Olivia had reached out to Saf in order to tell her about a treatment clinic in Singapore. It turned out that our situations were quite similar. Like us, Olivia had been told there was nothing that medics in the UK could do for her son, Oscar, but thanks to this treatment – called CAR-T therapy – he was still alive.

Her message had come in, I think, around February-March time, and so during that period at home, as well as keeping our fingers crossed that Azaylia's cancer might somehow retreat, we'd been exploring that as an option.

We'd been exploring other options too. I dare say that between the two of us we had explored every avenue going. In particular, I had worked hard to get hold of a chemo drug called venetoclax, which was not available in this country – not until I made some calls and established that there were, in fact, supplies of it in the UK, at which point we got it released for Azaylia's use.

So there was all that going on in the background. We were exploring different drugs, with different pharmaceutical companies, which was an exhausting, soul-sapping business, especially because there were so many dead ends.

Not only that, but of the various alternatives open to us, nothing was what we really wanted, which was an actual cure, something that might eradicate the cancer for good. In that respect, this CAR-T therapy was the only game in town.

There were three countries offering CAR-T therapy treatments: China, the US and Singapore. China was out of the question for Covid reasons and clinics in the US wouldn't treat anyone under the age of two. That left Singapore, which was able to boast great results with the therapy, even with patients of Azaylia's age, but would need to do something called a haploidentical, or haplo, transplant, which is a bone marrow transplant derived from blood and stem cells donated by a close biological match. The difference in this case – and what distinguished the haplo transplant from the stem cell transplant she'd already had – was that the clinic in Singapore preferred to work with a half-match, which meant that either me or Saf could be donors.

Having registered Azaylia into the clinic and discussed it over Zoom with a professor in Singapore – things moving pretty fast – they had already suggested that the donor should be me, and that once the transplant had been successful, they would work on CAR-T therapy for Azaylia's leukaemia cells. What differentiates CAR-T therapy from chemo is that it doesn't wipe out the whole body; it's specially targeted therapy which will attack specific cells.

At the same time as we were having our Zoom meetings,

we were checking things out with consultants in the UK and were satisfied that the clinic in Singapore was reputable and trustworthy.

Not only that, but our medical team in the UK was more than happy to work with them in order to prepare Azaylia for the procedure. Before making the journey she would need to have blood samples taken in order to send off to the clinic. She would also need a blood transfusion, chemotherapy with two separate drugs – one of them the venetoclax that I had so painstakingly sourced – and bone marrow samples, again to send off to Singapore.

Once in Singapore, we would likely be there for at least a year, maybe even two at the outside.

Oh, and one other thing: it was going to cost a million quid.

CHAPTER 43

As if the current obstacles weren't enough, another fly in the ointment was that we wouldn't be allowed to travel together as a family. No prizes for guessing why. Yes, Covid.

There was no way we could stomach not being out there as a family, so the strategy we came up with was for Saf and Azaylia to travel out first. In Singapore, Azaylia would undergo tests and preparations for a period of around three weeks before I joined them, the idea being that as the donor they couldn't refuse me entry to the country, and we'd all be together.

The thought terrified us. What if something happened on the plane? What if Azaylia was upset and I wasn't there? How was I going to be able to go three weeks without seeing her at home?

We had to put our fears to one side and concentrate on the big prize. It was pretty much go-time. We had consent from

Birmingham Children's Hospital; we had approval, consent and acceptance from the clinic in Singapore. It was just a case of raising the money. With this in mind, we decided to turn to our supporters, and on 28 March 2021, we announced an appeal on social media:

After long discussions and a global outreach for treatment, our consultants along with consultants from around the world have come to the conclusion that the ONLY option to save Azaylia's life is to fly to Singapore for CAR-T therapy plus a haplo transplant, for a minimum period of 1 year. Because of the aggressiveness of Azaylia's disease, we don't have time on our side and we may have to fly out within a matter of weeks. This treatment and associated expenses will be in excess of 1 million pounds with an initial deposit of £500,000 just to be accepted into the hospital and onto the program.

Azaylia is such a strong little girl who has fought through every near-impossible battle so far and she has done it all with love in her heart and a smile on her face! We pray that we can raise the funds to get her to Singapore so she can continue fighting for the life that she loves so much! ♡

Azaylia has changed our lives, she has made our lives, and she deserves the chance to live her own life. She is beautiful, she is strong, she is courageous and she glows with hope and happiness. Our hearts are intertwined and with one beat of her heart, our hearts beat along together. Please help our hearts continue to beat as one! ♡

We are on our knees asking for help to get us to Singapore. Even the smallest of donations can help us reach our goal! Please help us to save our beautiful daughter, Azaylia, she has inspired not only us as her parents but so many other people around the world. If you have been following our journey you can see that she shows us all every day how much she loves life and wants to be here! ♡

Please save this post. Please share this post. And please help us to save our beautiful little girl!

By now, Azaylia was a national story. I would get hundreds of thousands of likes on any post on Instagram. One film I posted around this time got 8.3 million views. We had had a piece on the ITV News, and the newspapers, especially *The Sun*, the *Daily Mirror* and the *Daily Mail*, regularly reported updates. We were lucky – blessed, in fact, that people had become invested in our story. We had the best representative ever, of course, in Azaylia, who even at her most poorly was capable of melting the hardest hearts. Photogenic doesn't even cover it. So we hoped that we could at least cover some of the costs using the appeal, and perhaps raise the rest 'in-house' as it were, by approaching individuals, calling in favours and so on.

What actually happened was that I accidentally published the text of the appeal the night before the official morning launch, but didn't share it, the idea being that it would be something people would see first thing slightly later that morning, just as I would be arriving at the *Good Morning Britain* studio on my own fundraising push – a cycle ride to give the campaign a boost. We just hoped that the public would respond.

And boy, did they respond. I was in hospital with Azaylia at the time, idly checking my phone that night, when I suddenly sat bolt upright, confronted by the fact that we had already raised £75,000.

This was something like twenty minutes after the appeal had gone up. And the tally kept on going up and up. Every time I checked my phone, the total had increased. It wasn't as if it was just creeping up either. It was shooting up, until literally within a few hours of publication we were at the halfway point.

From there it only continued to climb. In twenty-four hours it was already at the target, making it the fastest-ever GoFundMe campaign to reach a million. Ultimately, we would reach £1.6 million.

Donors were from all over. As well as thousands upon thousands of supporters and followers, we had support and donations from Umar Kamani, the co-founder of PrettyLittleThing, who gave £20,000, Mrs Hinch, Adam Frisby of In The Style, Molly-Mae Hague and Maura Higgins of *Love Island*, as well as Kate and Rio Ferdinand.

With the donations came thousands of supportive messages – well-wishers telling us how much they had been inspired by Azaylia and her story. It was a true marker of the effect she had on those who saw her story. They couldn't help but be invested. We used to say things to her like, 'You're amazing. You did this.' And it was absolutely true. She did. The power of Azaylia's personality. The inspiring example of her strength.

It reached across boundaries and crossed the age divide. People knew that little girl deserved a chance. They wanted her to live.

Watching the total increase hour by hour gave rise to moments of sheer euphoria. I swear to God that we had honestly expected the GoFundMe campaign to be something that ticked over in the background while we raised the money internally, and needless to say we'd been sweating the possible delay: what if it took us a while to raise the rest of the money and it became too late? Time was very much of the essence. The one thing we knew about Azaylia's hateful disease was that it didn't hang around. It was aggressive. It was fast.

But suddenly, there it was. The whole lot. Every single penny and more. And we were riding a wave of jubilation, running around making arrangements. We took a picture of Azaylia for her passport. We started booking flights, making plans.

We had hope then. Not just hope but *hope*. And yes, of course I was old enough and ugly enough to realise that a moment of euphoria this intense is often followed by, well, the dreaded bang, and that when it came to Azaylia, those bangs were very loud and very distressing indeed, but I didn't think about that. Negative thoughts went against the Club 100 vibe. I just got on with the job of getting Azaylia to Singapore.

We made preparations for her to go into surgery for another bone marrow test. The aim of this was that samples of cerebral spinal fluid and blood could be sent to Singapore via a special 48-hour delivery service in order that they could begin tests and create CAR-T treatment for the disease. They literally planned to tailor the treatment specifically to her.

At the same time, back in the UK, our consultants would be working out a short course of chemotherapy in order to bring her into remission.

The following day, 31 March, Azaylia was yet again given anaesthetic and taken into theatre for the sample extraction, blood transfusion and then, later, chemotherapy. It was awful to witness, but something we felt we had to put her through, knowing it was for the greater good.

As the day wore on, though, came another blow. Consultants discovered that leukaemia was forming in Azaylia's cerebral spinal fluid, putting her at risk of it finding its way to the brain. This meant that she would have to have chemotherapy intrathecally, through the spinal tap, in order to attack the leukaemia but protect her brain. In order to check that was safe, she'd need a CT scan on her head.

By now, Saf and I felt like two people being buffeted by the winds of fortune. One moment we were celebrating a wildly successful fundraising campaign, the next we were having to watch as our baby endured what was possibly the worst day of medical procedures yet – and with more to come.

Did we, in our darkest moments, wonder whether this course of action was the right one? No, we didn't. After all, did I want to wake up one day thinking, *I didn't do enough? We didn't try this, we didn't try that.* No. Not going to happen. If we were going down, we wanted to go down swinging. Azaylia was a fighter, and on her behalf we would fight.

By then we'd had just three or so hours of sleep in two days. We were of course used to the fatigue – exhaustion had been our life for months and months on end. I'd forgotten what a good night's sleep felt like. But the tempo of the whole situation seemed to have suddenly increased, making us as exhausted mentally as we were physically. As I said over social media, 'If you asked me a year ago I would never imagine how strong I could or would have to be. That being said, you never really know how strong you are until being strong is your only option.'

The quote was from Bob Marley, whose 'Buffalo Soldier' Azaylia and I would often dance to. Exactly the inspiration I needed at a time like that.

And then?

Bang.

Bang, bang, BANG.

CHAPTER 44

The test results had come back. I don't really know where to start. The results were simply a list of terrible, heart-breaking news, all of it adding up to the same thing.

Firstly, the CT scan on Azaylia's head had revealed two large leukaemia tumours on her brain. You remember that it was planned for Azaylia to have her chemotherapy intrathecally, effectively in order to protect the brain? The tumours made that no longer an option.

All told, the sheer severity of her condition meant that she only had one, maybe two days to live. She might not even survive the night.

We had heard this before, of course. We had heard it before and watched as our beautiful daughter defied the doctors and lived to fight not just another day, but days and weeks and months. I had danced around a hospital room with a baby girl the doctors said was a miracle.

But that didn't make it easier. Knowing she'd beaten the

odds before didn't make it a foregone conclusion that she'd do it again, no matter how positive we stayed – and we did, we really did – no matter how much hope we hung onto. The hope and positivity is what stops you crumpling to the floor and curling up in a foetal position. But you still wander through the hours feeling like a drone.

That night, she stayed in hospital, and she did indeed survive the night. The next day, we took her home accompanied by a palliative care team. Into our home came oxygen tanks and monitors, and we were told to prepare for the worst.

Still we weren't finished yet. The fight wasn't done. Watching over Azaylia at home, we became aware that something wasn't quite right with her. Now I know that seems a ludicrous thing to say given what she was going through, but I'm talking relatively speaking here. She seemed to us a bit ... what's the word? A bit 'medicated', and so at home we decided to reduce the pain relief, just a little.

The next day she was much sharper, almost as bright as a button, and that change sparked a little bit of a fire beneath us. The very same day we returned to the hospital and requested a meeting with the consultant.

Once again, I was in assertive mode. Not rude. Not threatening. Just forthright. 'There are two kinds of people in this world,' I told them. 'There are people who when confronted with a problem have a fight mechanism, and there are people who have a flight mechanism. Neither one is wrong or right, but they're the two kinds of people.

'Me, I've always been a fighter, and I always will be a fighter. My daughter is a product of me through nature via nurture, and that means she'll be a fighter, too.

'A lot of people might feel more comfortable being at home with their kid. They think that being in a hospital or on a flight to Singapore might break them. But it would break me to stay at home knowing my daughter's dying and I'm not doing anything about it. We only have one chance at life and I want to make sure that we're doing everything we can possibly do to preserve it, because when you're gone, you're gone. She's fought hard to fight all the way through; I want to honour that by giving her the best chance at surviving.'

What choice did they have? None, really. It was back to the drawing board and for three or four days we pushed and fought for options. We forced them to consider other chemotherapy drugs, and we were especially keen to try radiotherapy, even though it's not usually given to children under a year old.

We were still holding out hope that we could bring her back into remission and reduce the tumours so that she was able to fly. Anything. Singapore was still very much on the table. If her cancer could be controlled and reduced just enough for her to be able to get on a plane then we had a chance at a cure.

In the meantime she was given an ultrasound scan, the results of which came back the next day, which was 8 April.

We hoped for good news.

We prayed for it.

And our prayers were ignored.

They had found more tumours. Azaylia had tumours in her stomach, spleen, lungs and kidneys. Her disease was that aggressive.

There was more. The consultant had received an email from Singapore. We always knew Azaylia was special, so it made sense that her disease would be unique, too. So much so that the clinic in Singapore was very sad to report that they would be unable to create a CAR-T therapy for her. In addition to that we were told that she wouldn't have been able to fly with the tumours on her brain anyway. The pressure of the flight would have had a catastrophic effect.

Once again, Azaylia was given days to live.

I was still swinging, telling them, 'We don't do problems any more, we do solutions,' but all the same I knew that we were at the end of the road. You can have all the mantras in the world, but they're nothing without options. You can have a positive mindset. You can have an optimistic outlook and a can-do attitude. But all the belief in the world counts for nothing if you don't have options.

If there's nothing you can do, then there's nothing you can do.

And there was nothing we could do.

CHAPTER 45

Feeling as though we were standing at the edge of the world looking down into a dark void below, we brought Azaylia home.

At home we had oxygen tanks and SATs machines (they're machines that monitor breathing, oxygen and heart rate). We still kept the house spotless, of course, but it was no longer so imperative. Before, when we'd placed her in her pushchair for walks, we needed to seal her up tight to protect her from outside germs, dust and so on. Again, that was no longer so essential. We could push her along in her pushchair and she could look out into the world – a world that we knew she would never see in its full glory, that she would never see without disease within her.

And now was when the cancer really made its presence felt. My mind went back to the previous October, how the onset of the disease from being at home to hospital and then intensive care had seemed so desperately rapid, almost as though the diagnosis itself had triggered it. Now it was the same. As if this barbaric disease had somehow been given permission to riot in her little body.

Up until then it had been more internal. The good Lord had seen fit not to allow the disease to wreak havoc on those beautiful, cherubic features. Now, though, even He had to admit defeat in the face of cancer, and just to see Azaylia was to see how very ill she was. Those times we'd had before, when we'd look at her, and say, 'Look at you, lickle lion, you're getting better, we can see it. Let's go, Champ,' seemed like a time of illusion, desperate parents kidding themselves. You could see now that the illness was tearing at her insides, ripping her apart.

I don't know what was the final straw. When the strong words failed me, and all the fight finally left me. Maybe it was then. Maybe it was looking at that tiny, precious little being ravaged by disease.

But okay, pull yourself together, Ashley. Do you want your daughter's last days on Earth to be a state of permanent darkness? Do you want her to look at her parents' faces and see sadness? There'll be a time for grief. There'll be a time to mourn. But that time isn't now. Right now we do everything we can to ensure that her lasting impression of life is one of love and joy. Let everyone hold her, let everyone kiss her, let everyone tell her how much they love her.

Things were different at home, no doubt. I knew it was the best place to be, given the terrible prognosis. Even so, there was a real 'safety net' aspect to being in hospital. There were people to ask for advice or whose behaviour and attitudes you could emulate. At home you're kind of *adrift*. The boundaries of what you might laughingly call my comfort zone had been expanding month by month, and now it was happening again. It was not lost on me that we had been allowed home in order for Azaylia to pass, but that was now the only certainty, that passing was imminent. I didn't know when. I didn't know how. I didn't know how to be, how to look after her.

When we had first arrived back home, the lights had been off and it was pitch-black. I had felt like I was moving in mud. Everything was achy. That feeling largely remained in the days to come. As much as events affected me mentally, they affected me physically too. Just standing up from the sofa was an effort. At night, when Saf and Azaylia would be upstairs, I stayed on the sofa, unable to confront the fear that if and when I slept, I might wake to find that Azaylia was no longer with us.

Often I had the company of my mum and sister, Alissia, both of whom had taken leave from work in order to create a family bubble and support us in those final days. It helped them because they got to hold and kiss Azaylia; it helped us because they made sure that we were looking after ourselves, eating properly and so on. I talked before about how me and Saf's fields of focus had shifted to Azaylia and how during the journey that focus had become even sharper and more defined. Over the months we'd been in hospital there had been bits of work that I simply had to attend to in order to keep putting food on the table, but mainly our world had been the hospital, consultants, nurses, treatment.

And now it had shrunk even more. Now it was simply Azaylia. Our absolute and only priority was making sure that the dark tunnel in which we found ourselves was invisible to her. With that in mind I took her out for walks, just like a normal daddy, and I commented to Saf after one particular walk how I had never felt at once so happy and so heart-broken. The heartbreak I kept well away from Azaylia. The happiness I shared.

That was also the priority of our family. Everybody came. My family, Saf's family, all of them wanting to make the most of their opportunity to pick up, hold and cuddle Azaylia. We kept things sensible, asking people outside the bubble to stay outside the house and stand at the door, limiting the numbers we had at any one time. Some of the measures were taken over Covid concerns, others because it would be tiring for Azaylia, not to mention emotionally draining for us.

She had been home for four days – every day, hour, minute, second a bonus – when word reached us of things going on in the world outside. We already knew that Azaylia's story had touched the lives of thousands, but now it was as though it had entered another level. The first thing was a message from The Rock – as in Dwayne 'The Rock' Johnson. One of his contacts had brought Azaylia's story to his attention and he'd taken the time to record a greeting, offering words of strength and support. That video, on my Instagram feed alone, has got almost 6.5 million views.

The next thing we knew, landmarks were lighting up orange, inspired by Azaylia in support of leukaemia awareness. Clacton Pier, Liverpool's Radio City Tower, Wembley Stadium, Newcastle's Millennium Bridge, Nuneaton Town Hall, Coventry's Whittle Arch, Blackpool Tower and the London Eye – all of them bathed in beautiful orange light displays organised by people affected by Azaylia's story, moved by a smile that could melt icebergs.

It started happening overseas too. Toronto's CN Tower went orange in support and, perhaps most impressively, so did Niagara Falls. It really is worth looking at the images online if you can. For us, to see Niagara Falls glowing orange, a gesture in support of our little girl, was beyond words.

Similarly, one day we stepped outside to see an aeroplane sky-writing a heart and the letter A for her. I looked around and could see that others had come out of their homes and were standing on the pavement and on the grass verges. The support and love we felt was something else. You don't realise until it happens, the strength that you get from it. True, it was no longer the strength to fight, now it was the strength to cope – but that was just as crucial.

There was a clap for Azaylia, too. People came out of their homes to clap for her, just as they had done for the NHS during the first lockdown. Loads of celebrities took part in the clap, and we had messages of support as well. Most touchingly, local residents came out to show their solidarity.

We had set up an email address to which people could send videos, and within two hours the inbox was full. That's just the people who bothered sending in a video. Tens of thousands more stood on their doorsteps for us. It meant – and still means – so much.

But even as these amazing, community-based things happened, we were watching Azaylia slip away. If you look at the video of the sky-writing, for example, you can see the disease on her face. Her eyes are puffy and closed, her skin is pale, nose scabby, mouth sore. Everything was swelling up.

Every step of the way with Azaylia, we had been forced to adapt to our new reality. We went from perfect brand-new baby to Azaylia with an NG tube up her nose. Now with wires. Now with a central line. Each time it was a bit of a shock, but one you dealt with, maybe because even with the wires and tubes, she always looked amazing.

But this was harder to take. There was no getting used to the puffy, closed-up eyes. She never stopped being our little girl. Just that she was a very, very poorly version of herself.

And as we *oohed* and *ahhed* and did our best to keep our spirits up for her sake, we were broken inside. There was no doubt about it now. She was going.

CHAPTER 46

I said that we entered our home without the safety net of hospital, wondering when Azaylia might pass and how to behave when she did. But the one question that had really played on our minds, was *how* – how would she pass?

It was something that the nurses had to explain to us. They told us Azaylia's body would slowly shut down. That one by one, her organs would fail. It was a process that involved the production of fluid, but because the organs were shutting down that fluid wouldn't be processed and would have nowhere to go. As a result, her eyes would swell shut. Blood would escape in her tears and in her nappy. As the days wore on, their grim predictions came to pass. We were seeing it happen to our little girl. We were watching the process in real time.

Towards the end, Azaylia had small transfusions in order to ease her discomfort, and at one stage the puffiness in her eyes reduced really quite dramatically. But these were temporary measures only. They were merely to help, not heal. We were way beyond that now. The fact that the nurses had moved her from Oramorph on to an even stronger type of morphine spoke volumes.

Morphine, I had thought, back in October. *Morphine*. I was in a new world where my baby needed morphine. Now – now she needed even stronger morphine.

Sometimes she seemed to perk up. There's a picture of me, my brother, Matty, Azaylia and Anaya that breaks my heart. Azaylia and Anaya are touching hands. It's hard to look at that picture and think that Azaylia's no longer here. That she never had a chance to properly meet her cousin. You hold onto those moments and, as I said, feel as happy and yet at the same time as heartbroken as you'll ever be. You want to scream frustration and anger at the sky. You want to break down and cry with the joy of life and the pain of grief. You wonder how the world could possibly contain such sorrow and anguish. You wonder at a world that can allow a little baby to bleed from her eyes when she blinks, bleed when she cries. What kind of sick and messed-up world allows that?

As the last days approached, when Azaylia was obviously fading, I took to fitfully dozing in a spare room or on the sofa, just to give mother and baby some space in the bedroom. Up until that point we'd been keeping her heart rate and oxygen-level monitors activated, and on occasion, when one or the other had dipped, we had had to summon help.

Now, however, Saf and I agreed that the monitors should stay off. It was evident that there was just one stage of Azaylia's life left, and that was her passing.

That night I didn't sleep in the spare room, I came to bed

to be with Azaylia. Since October, I had taken to hating the night. I feared sleep because if I fell asleep with Azaylia awake, I might wake up to find her gone. Those times I've described, when I'd wake up and the first thing I saw was Azaylia, looking at me, smiling at me: the relief of seeing her there, and the joy. It wasn't just her smile, although that was reward enough. It was the knowledge that she was alive, that the day ahead would contain Azaylia.

I didn't know if I could handle whatever the opposite of that was.

And it had been the same at home. Sleep was fear. Sleep was the unknown.

But that night I came to bed, and Saf and I lay with Azaylia between us. Downstairs, my mum and Alissia had the sofas as beds.

The household slept. One of us for the last time.

We woke the next morning, almost in unison. I learned later that Saf had felt the same as me, which was that Azaylia was to be gathered up that day. She had gone downstairs and said to my mum and sister, 'This is it, this is the day.'

Upstairs, I woke to find that Azaylia's breathing was laboured and shallow.

'We should ring,' I said, and either my mum or my sister rang the palliative care team. They also reached out to Saf's brother, Danny, with whom she's really close.

And I lay with Azaylia, face to face, hearing her breathe. I knew what was happening, but at the same time, I could not understand it. I knew that life was ending. That I was about to experience the greatest-ever loss. I knew that things would never be the same again.

I took our little girl's hand. I told her, 'It's okay, baby, it's okay,' listening to her life ebb away, watching her poorly puffed-up eyes flicker and close.

Saf was back in the room. She was working on one of the machines to try and check Azaylia's stats.

In the bed, still facing Azaylia, I began counting. I was counting the pauses between her breaths, like this ...

'One, two ...'

Breath.

'One, two, three, four ...'

Breath.

'One, two, three, four, five ...'

Until I was up to twelve. And that was it. There were no more breaths.

Part Five

LET'S GO, CHAMP

CHAPTER 47

It must've been some time. People had entered the room. The palliative care team had arrived. My mum, Alissia and Saf's brother Danny were there. Saf and I lay on either side of Azaylia, cradling her in bed, the three of us together as a family – the way it was, and the way it should have been.

There was the sound of crying in the room. Was it me? I'm not sure, but what I do remember is that without warning, I was suddenly in the grip of a horrific physical reaction.

I now know that it was nothing more serious than a panic attack, but at the time the effect was as dramatic as it was traumatic. I began palpitating and twitching. Vaguely, I heard Saf calling for help, and thank God for the nurses who came to me and were able to administer oxygen.

I was okay. The whole episode was a mercifully short and thankfully minor sideshow. Even so, I look back on it with shame. Having gone through the process and been a tower of strength at every stage, I felt as though I had let myself and my family down at the last minute.

Not that I was thinking that way at the time. In the immediate aftermath of her passing, as a kind of fog seemed to settle over the room and over everybody in it – over the whole house, in fact – I went into something approaching a catatonic state. I literally shut off from everyone. As the last breath left her tiny body, things simply stopped making sense to me. Nobody could say anything that might help or take the pain away. It was like every instrument inside me was smashed. There were no readings any more.

During that day and in the days ahead, I had dark thoughts. Among other things, I thought about the trade I'd make just to have my daughter back. I'd think, *You can take my whole family away, just don't take her.* I'd think that I could cope with losing them all, every single one, just give Azaylia back to me. During those times I would wonder about my ability to cope. The pain felt like a knife going into me, over and over again.

Losing a parent's not easy. I had to deal with that possibility relatively recently when my dad was diagnosed with cancer, thankfully a situation that is now past. To have lost him would have been hard. It was hard losing my paternal grandmother, Grandma Cain, who passed away while I was out of the country making *SAS: Who Dares Wins*. But if a parent or grandparent goes, you have the comfort of knowing that it's within the established order of things. In a way, your whole life is spent preparing for that eventuality. It's the way it should be.

When you father a child, you don't anticipate outliving that child. You expect them to be giving the eulogy at *your* funeral, not the other way around. So what eats you up in a situation like that is the injustice of it; the unfairness of not being able to look back and think of all the great times you had together, because there weren't enough of them.

With Azaylia, we made sure that we brought what joy we could into her life. But it wasn't enough, because she was only in this world for eight months, and in those eight months she was riddled with cancer. And that's what hurts, that's what really pains me.

The shock immediately following her passing was so numbing I'm not sure there were any thoughts running through my head, but if they did then it was that feeling – that feeling of unfairness.

I remember there being family around. I remember music playing, *I Wan'na be Like You. Oobee-do.*

I remember silence, also. And I remember that everything ached. My head, eyes, body, and especially my heart, which was heavy with heartbreak and irreparably damaged. It seemed as though I had been transported through a portal into another dimension where everything moved in half time and nothing made sense. Not the TV, not other people, not even myself.

Those parts of me that existed before Azaylia, before even Saf, felt as if they belonged to someone else. It's only while writing this book that I remember certain aspects of my life, and only then because I've forced myself to do it, as though my brain's hard drive had just enough memory for things to do with Azaylia and the rest of it had been backed up somewhere. For eight months that was me. I was not Ashley Cain, ex-footballer, reality TV star. All that stuff was in the Cloud. I was just that one word: 'Dadda'.

I remember the family arriving to say their farewells.

And music playing. So many tears shed. I was functioning. Moving. Giving and receiving hugs. I held Azaylia and watched as other people kissed and cuddled her, but that feeling of numbness, of moving through some thick and viscous substance never left me. The darkness swirled around me.

At some point my mate Danny from the funeral directors arrived, and I give thanks to him now, for being there and being such a solid rock of support. Azaylia was removed to the funeral directors and placed in the Chapel of Rest. There she would remain for around a month – Covid having caused havoc and delays in that industry just as much as it had everywhere else – and so we would go and see her, read to her, take her toys and play music.

Saf in particular was keen to go several times a day to the Chapel of Rest. I can't say I went as much as she did; I was struggling with issues around thoughts of Azaylia passing over. I was wondering, *Is she still in the house with us? Would she be wondering where her mummy and daddy were going? Why they were leaving her?*

I didn't know whether Azaylia had left yet, where she was, or if she was looking down on us. Did I imagine it, or did I really feel her presence?

I wouldn't have long to wait to get my answer.

A week or so after she passed, I pulled on a pair of trainers – an orange pair I'd bought especially, in order to mark new beginnings – and I went running. The run went well, so I went out again a few days later. I'd taken to drinking a fair bit during this time, a fact that I knew in my heart of hearts I would soon need to address. But even with a banging whisky hangover, I was still managing to pull on the shoes and hit the road. I won't say that anything helped with the all-consuming grief, certainly not the booze, but of everything I did, running was the most beneficial.

As the days went on, and I went running more, I found myself looking up to the skies. Increasingly what I saw were the most beautiful, brilliant orange skies. Saf and I would see rainbows too. In the coming days and weeks we would see them often. One particular occasion, just two days before her funeral (a day that we had decided to call 'Azaylia's Day'), the entire sky was lit up orange, the most vivid, vibrant, breath-taking orange you can possibly imagine. It made the local news, on which they described it as a 'fire sky'.

But Saf and I knew different. We knew that Azaylia was sending us a message.

During Azaylia's illness, fitness was practically my only means of staying sane. I used to run in Birmingham, but I guess I was too wrapped up in the trauma of the situation to take much notice of my surroundings. Suddenly I was seeing. *Really seeing*. More and more, my eyes were drawn upwards and the sky would be orange, and I'd know that Azaylia was watching. As a result, I took to training outside whenever possible so that I could feel close to her.

Perhaps, just as she ushered me out of doors and urged me to look to the skies, she also guided my thoughts, for my mind went to the charity Saf and I had talked about starting in her name.

We weren't able to save Azaylia's life. But perhaps Azaylia could save the lives of others.

CHAPTER 48

Recently, I was asked a hypothetical question, and it was this: If an orange glow appeared in the garden and by walking into the glow I could meet Azaylia again, but I would instantly disappear forever, would I do it? Would I take my leave from this Earth?

The answer: I'd jump out the window.

'Really, Ashley?' they said. 'Would you? All the good work you're doing in her memory. All the money you're raising for leukaemia and for other children suffering just like her? It would all cease.'

No. Same answer. You wouldn't even hear me say goodbye. I'd be gone and I don't think anybody would hold that against me. If, like in the Kate Bush song, I could make a deal with God, it would be to have just one more dance with her, just to let me feel that feeling again, just once. Just one song.

But that's not going to happen. And because there's

no orange glow, and there never will be a deal with God, I've instead made it my purpose to achieve on Earth every-thing that I can. And I'm going to do that knowing that if Azaylia could go through everything she went through and still be smiling, then I could take that belief, confidence, courage and strength and know that there is no challenge I am not capable of.

That's why we started the charity. It was actually an idea that we'd been kicking around for some time. We'd been so touched by what we'd seen on Ward 18 and Ward 19 of Birmingham Children's Hospital, so moved by the hundreds and thousands of messages that we had received on social media, that in the end it was almost a no-brainer. We knew that whatever happened with Azaylia – even if she'd lived – we wanted to set up a charity in her name so that, in this world or the next, she could help other children in her position.

Talks moved up a gear shortly after her passing. You know me enough by now to know that I need to be *doing* something. Need to be moving. And whether that was physically moving, by training or running, or metaphorically by making moves for the future, then it had to be done.

As early as 8 May 2021 – just under a fortnight before Azaylia's Day – we shared an update on our GoFundMe page in which we pledged that some of the money raised in the appeal to send Azaylia to Singapore would be used to give her 'a magical and deserving send-off – something we believe that you would all want to be a part of', and that the remaining money would be used as starting capital for the new charity we were setting up in her name.

That charity became The Azaylia Foundation. It was

officially launched at the end of August 2021, which, as we told ITV's *Lorraine*, was just in time for World Childhood Cancer Awareness Month in September.

We began the Foundation with a mission statement – 'fearless in the fight against children's cancer' – and a commitment to battle childhood cancer by advancing practices of early diagnosis as well as wanting to help develop new treatment in the UK. I guess that in many ways our aim was to be a slightly disruptive technology in the field. We wanted to shake things up. When we investigated the field of childhood cancer more thoroughly, our focus widening from Azaylia to other children in the same situation, we discovered that there are five new cases of cancer diagnosed in under fifteen-year-olds *every day*. Four deaths a week. I'd always been led to believe that childhood cancer is a rarity. I don't know about you, but that doesn't feel especially rare to me.

And the next thing we learned was that despite, or should I say because of, this whole rare-not-rare thing, childhood cancer receives less than 3 per cent of overall cancer funding. Yes, I know I said this at the beginning of the book, but it bears repeating. The lack of funds going into the childhood cancer space means that you get a parallel lack of investment, and if you don't get investment, you don't get growth.

What we are promoting at the Foundation is working towards gentler, more child-focused treatments, towards training GPs and staff in order to spot cancer in children early. (Can't bang the drum enough on this: early diagnosis, early diagnosis. It's what it's all about.)

What we also knew was that to fix this problem we needed to challenge and change the perception of childhood cancer in government, in institutions, in the media and, of course, in the public at large.

It wasn't necessarily easy to arrive at that remit. Brainstorming ideas originally, we had wanted to do a variety of things that, in the end, we had to reluctantly set to one side. We had considered providing financial support to families seeking treatment, or perhaps creating magical experiences for children in hospitals. In the end, and with the help of the Charities Commission and dozens of experts in the field of childhood cancer and charity oversight, we decided that what we needed to do was address the bigger picture. That's why we chose to target the root cause (early diagnosis, changing the system, changing perception) and will work with any organisations that also have that as their aim.

(Just as an aside, although it's not the main thrust of our work, we do donate towards the individual treatment of children, when that treatment is not covered by the NHS – and I'm personally involved with raising money in that field – but it tends to be on a case-by-case basis. If it's something you need, please go to The Azaylia Foundation's website https://theazayliafoundation.com/. You can find a bit more information at the end of the book, too.)

Since the Foundation's inception we've become partnered with some incredible institutions. We've got a CEO, passionate parents, leading practitioners, oncologists and pharma people on board, and in the first year of the Foundation we were able to donate money to help fund multiple trials at Great Ormond Street Hospital and Birmingham Children's Hospital – trials that advance diagnosis and treatment availability. We've also bought equipment and set up the Azaylia PhD fund, which aims to find clinicians and researchers to go further into the paediatrics side of things so that we're putting new talent into that space. So not only do we supply funding to get big brains in there, but then we fund research and trials to keep them in there.

The point being that we always have an end goal. We are not a foundation that just gives away money to the right people; we want to give away money to the right people in the sure knowledge that there is a path to follow and a goal to reach.

As trustees and founders, Saf and I are intimately involved and work tirelessly for the charity and are constantly amazed by the things it achieves.

I decided also that there was something that I could do to really super-size my contribution to the Foundation, and that goes back firstly to my abiding passion – fitness – but also to Azaylia and the promise I made to her on her day.

CHAPTER 49

I do take solace from the fact that I was able to spend so much time with Azaylia during her short time on Earth. I speak to so many parents going through a similar thing, and I say to them, 'Just be present in every moment. Make the most of every single second of your day with your child.'

Somebody who hasn't been in my situation might look at a statement like that and think that I'm only saying it because I know about loss, but actually I'm not. I'm saying it because that time with Azaylia was the best time I ever had, and the best time I will ever have. It was the most magical period of my life, and if I could do it again – complete with illness, yes, really – I'd do it again. Which is why I say it. Not because I believe that the end is bleak and will end in darkness, just because even if you're among the lucky ones, that will still be the defining moment of you and your child's life.

But still ... Nobody should have to say goodbye to their child.

That injustice I was talking about. The sense of unfairness. It never leaves you. It partners your grief and accompanies you everywhere. You can't outrun it, and believe me, I tried. Around this time – by which I mean the time of Azaylia's farewell, Azaylia's Day – I was going out running quite a bit, just not as consistently as I do now, and probably not even as consistently as I did when we were at the hospital, when I used to leave the hotel and run along the canal.

And the reason that I wasn't running quite as often as I really needed to was because I had another release. And that release was alcohol.

I've already touched on it, but by now, I was drinking every night. Whisky. I'd love to say that the drink somehow numbed the grief, or 'took the edge off', as they say, but I don't think it did really. In fact, if anything, I found that I was more emotional when I was drinking. Perhaps it served a purpose, in that I was able to express my emotions, although these days I would advocate being able to do that without the need for alcohol. I just found myself less able to contain the grief when I'd been drinking. And worse, of course, I would wake up in the morning feeling terrible. I'd tell myself, *Not again tonight. I don't want to feel this way again tomorrow morning.*

But then the evening would roll around, and I'd reach for the bottle again, a little voice calling out to me to have a drink even though I'd promised myself I wouldn't. That's when you know that things are getting out of hand. When you're doing it despite yourself. When you're doing it even though you know you shouldn't. I'd tell myself that I 'needed' it. I'd tell myself that it helped me sleep, when what it actually did was knock me out and what sleep I got was disturbed and fitful. I wasn't on the slippery slope but I could see the slippery slope in the near distance.

The thing was, I was panic-stricken grief-central during the daytime. On edge, my mind whirring, thinking of what we'd been through. Thinking of Azaylia's passing, where she was now. Thinking of how to plan her day. The day was approaching, and you're designing a casket. You're visiting the Chapel of Rest. You're thinking about the clothes she's to be buried in. You're wondering should she be buried or cremated? You're thinking what songs to play. Who to invite. How many cars do we need?

And for me, mainly, I was thinking about the eulogy I would have to give.

You don't have to do one, Ashley. Why put yourself through that?

Forget that. That's not an option. If I didn't speak about my daughter on her day then I would never, ever have been able to forgive myself. And to speak, I needed something to say. I needed to say something worthy of the occasion. I needed words that would resonate beyond the day itself.

Writing her eulogy became a pivotal moment in helping me find my way out of a hole that I'd not exactly fallen into, rather had sunk into. A hole that was, thanks to the booze, at least partly of my own making.

Having that job got me thinking about grief. It got me thinking how grief is a crazy journey that's unique to everybody who embarks upon it. You go through different aspects of it every day. What's through this grief-door? Oh, it's this feeling. I didn't expect that. What's through this new grief-door that

I'd never seen before? Oh, it's something new, a new feeling I've never felt before. I didn't expect that.

Writing the eulogy was yet another one of those doors. Perhaps it was a welcome one in the sense that it forced me to confront my grief, and I guess that I needed to do that, rather than try to numb it with whisky.

On the other hand, it was hard. It was hard to summon the words, which came from deep inside of me; hard to give them life and write them down. And when it came to contemplating the delivery? Imagine possibly the most pressured situation you can possibly have. I've been in a few of them. But I knew that nothing would ever compare to this. This was going to be the second saddest day of my life, where I would be at my lowest, most in pain and vulnerable. I had to stand and deliver a speech to a crowd, one that would do my daughter justice.

To do that, to even begin thinking about that, I had to revisit Azaylia, who she was and what she taught me. A bit like writing this book, I was forced to look back, and looking back, I was reminded again not only what a wonderful person Azaylia was, but what a wonderful time we had together.

I thought to myself, 'Do you know what? This can't stop now. This *cannot stop now*. Her journey is not over.' No – that's not right. What I should really say is, *Our journey together is not over*. I realised that my life with my daughter, fun though it was, had been restricted to a room in a hospital. I said to myself, 'That ain't right.'

I also started thinking about the film *Coco*. In *Coco*, what happens is that when people are forgotten about on Earth, they disappear in heaven. That helped me, too. I realised that I wanted as many people as I could in this world to know my daughter's name. I knew I would carry her name always. I knew that I would speak about her all the time. I want everyone in the world to know my daughter's name so that she's always remembered and always stays alive in heaven, so that her moments on this Earth far surpass mine, and that it's the same up there.

Azaylia's Day was heart-breaking. I put myself under so much pressure. I knew that she would be watching, and I thought to myself, *What kind of father does she want to see?* She wants to see her dad be strong and proud. Be upset, yes, but also lead the way and provide support for everyone around us. For that reason I put pressure on myself, and I believe that day set up the rest of my life. Why? Because I've taken the way that I felt that day – the way that I behaved and conducted myself – I've taken it and I've carried it forward into the work I've done with the Foundation, with the Ultra Challenges and my Christmas challenges (I now complete challenges every Christmas period to fundraise for those who need it) and now my work in the mental health space. It's made me the man I am today.

Tens of thousands of people lined the streets that day. I remember feeling the raw emotion that came off the crowd in waves and being almost literally supported by it, as though it was helping me stay on my feet, keeping my head from dropping. The sadness was there. The grief you could feel in the air. But you know what? There was also so much love. There was pure and true love for a little girl that none of them even knew, but whose life had touched theirs.

It's like the Queen. You knew about her. You knew of her influence and how she was the longest-running monarch. But for me, and maybe for many people of my generation, I didn't appreciate what effect she'd had on the world until I watched her funeral in September 2022. I was there all day watching it, transfixed by it, in awe of it all.

I'm not comparing the two, but Azaylia's Day had that same effect on me. For six to ten miles of Azaylia's parade, from the end of our road onwards, the streets were lined with people. I said tens of thousands back then and I really don't think it's an exaggeration: I mean, we'd been thinking that if it had been a nice summer's day, a few might turn up, but it wasn't a nice day, it was raining – and they still came.

Azaylia was taken to the service in a beautiful white Cinderella carriage pulled by white horses. As a family we walked for the first half a mile or so of the parade, me and Saf up front, and then went the rest of the way by car. It was important, that walk. Symbolic. As well as expressing our grief on the day, we also wanted to show strength.

I remember vividly sitting in the car, I had a horrible gut-wrenching feeling, I was feeling really, really low. Second to losing her, that day was the most difficult because we were saying goodbye for the last time. I was finding it hard to understand that Azaylia was no longer with us. It was hard to get to grips with the idea that we were burying our child, and from that day, we would never see her, we would never touch her. We were never going to be able to kiss or hug her. It was so difficult to grasp.

But I remember looking up out of the car window and seeing the crowds, how men, women and children were all in tears. You know what? They stood strong. And to see how much love there was for Azaylia was really warming. A mad part of grief is that you feel like not only have you lost that person but that the person is forgotten. When you lose someone, you feel as though you're the only person feeling sad.

But on that day, everyone was sad. The sky was sad. Tens of thousands of people lining the streets were all heartbroken, which magnified how much Azaylia was going to be missed in this world. I can't say it made it any easier, but I was grateful that so many people were able to be there at that moment and share so much sadness and heartbreak.

It was hard for me to take it in. On that day I wanted a worthy send-off for her. All the things she'd done in the world – even now I get people messaging me about how they became stem-cell donors because of her. She deserved a good send-off, and I'm pleased to say that we gave her that. I just needed to be brave.

The song I played for her at the service was 'Go the Distance' by Michael Bolton. As for my eulogy, well, you know the expression 'choking back tears'? I'm not even sure I knew what that meant until I stepped up that day.

'I think that when you have a child, as a parent, you can be slightly biased,' I started, 'but I think it's safe to say, on behalf of myself, my partner, to my friends and family and the whole world who have followed our story, that my daughter, Azaylia Diamond Cain, was special.

'Beautiful, strong, courageous and so, so inspirational. I don't think that a single person in this room can say they are too wise, too educated or experienced to have learned something from my lickle lion.

'From the second she came into my life everything changed. She changed my life, she saved my life and she made my life.

'What a strong and powerful journey, it is only now that I have taken a step back that I have actually realised how impactful it was.'

I remember having to stop to gather myself, thinking, *Come on, Ash, you got this.*

I was keen to ensure that I evoked memories of the little baby I knew, saying, 'I miss smelling her head. I miss blowing raspberries on her belly, I miss putting her feet on my face and going, "Poo, stinky feet!" She used to love that.

'I miss kissing her lips, even though Saf used to say, "Leave her alone," I'd say, "I can't," and I used to kiss her and kiss her and kiss her.

'I miss dancing with her, something we used to do every single day. I think the thing I really miss the most is, when we were in hospital, I used to stay most nights in hospital and I really, really, really miss waking up in the morning, opening the blinds and seeing her massive, massive beautiful smile.

'I used to be tired, probably only having an hour or two hours' sleep, I used to wake up in the morning and look over to my right and she would be there awake, not crying, not screaming, just waiting for me to wake up.

'As soon as I opened those blinds and said, "Hey baby" her feet were like this and her hands were going, it was the most beautiful thing.

'I used to get the music on straight away and I think we used to have the time of our lives every morning in that hospital.

'She was amazing and no matter what she went through, she always had a smile on her face, she always did it with grace and beauty.'

Wanting to acknowledge the effect she had on us as a family,

I continued, 'When Azaylia came along, I think we all looked at ourselves, realised what we had got, saw what we should be appreciating, put aside everything that needed to be put aside and came together as one.

'I think, as a family, we are all better because of Azaylia. I think during the time, I thought, if we stay strong, happy and positive, then she will be strong, happy and positive.

'As much as we can take some credit, truthfully it turned out that we gained our strength from her.

'We smiled because she smiled, we were brave because she was so fearless and we were strong because she was a true beacon of strength.

'She inspired us, she inspires you, she inspired everyone that followed her journey. In the end, this lickle lion that we thought we needed to love and be strong for had enough love and strength embedded in her to fuel the entire world.'

And of course I had to mention the film *Coco*, which, I said, 'turns to Mexican traditions to offer a more optimistic view on one's journey to heaven, that a journey to the other side should not be viewed as some unavoidable terror but as a remembrance to treasure our loved ones, both living and the heavenly. As long as our loved ones are remembered here on Earth, they will live on for eternity in paradise.

'So that being said, I made a promise to my daughter and myself that I will make her name live on. I will carry her name to the stars, I will be her vessel and help other families and poorly children until it is my final journey and then, hopefully then, I will be at peace, I will be happy as I will have earned my place in heaven, where I will be with you, my baby, once again.'

And now I ended on the note that in many ways has defined my life from that moment on. I said, 'To the top of every mountain, to the bottom of every valley, along every road, across every ocean, north to south, east to west, corner to corner, pillar to post, I will take you there, baby – let's go, Champ.

'My champion, my world, my hero – Azaylia Diamond Cain – I love you.'

CHAPTER 50

Afterwards, I reflected on that time we had at home, during Azaylia's final days. We had almost three weeks more than the doctors had predicted. Three weeks. Imagine that. What a miracle she was. Every step she took, she made it into a little miracle.

First diagnosed in October 2020, they said she wouldn't last a week: she did.

They told us that the chemotherapy might kill her: she nailed it.

She might not engraft: she did.

It might take a year. She did it in just over a month.

Probably not 100 per cent. But she did it.

And it's yet another of those things I learned from her. That stubbornness. That 'never say never' attitude. Yet another of those attributes I wanted to take forward into the challenges. Writing and saying the words of the eulogy, it cemented something in me. I thought to myself, *I don't want to be a man of false promises and hollow words. I want to be the guy who comes through. The guy who turns up.* From the moment of Azaylia's Day onward, I was no longer doing things for me, I was doing things for her. I was a man on a mission, and not planning to stop until that mission was complete – and until I join Azaylia in heaven, it never will be.

It didn't happen right away though. Not immediately. It must have been a few days after her funeral that I woke up with the usual feelings of alcoholic regret, except they were tinged with something else.

Shame.

Shame born not of the hangover but a shame that by drinking, I was letting Azaylia down, that I was disrespecting her legacy. I wanted to take Azaylia around the world and make her proud. I wanted to be the best I could be. No matter how much comfort I was getting from the booze (and let's face it, it was only a temporary kind of comfort anyway, no matter how much of a respite when all was said and done), I just wasn't the man I wanted to be. Not the man Azaylia deserved.

And I remember lying there, feeling embarrassed and ashamed and that I was nothing to be proud of, how those skies would stop turning orange unless I seriously bucked up my ideas. I thought of her and I thought of the kids on Ward 18.

Those kids are battling cancer while I'm feeling sorry for myself? What is my problem compared to theirs? What is my problem compared to the effort I plan to make on her behalf, the mountain ahead of me that I have to climb?

Don't get me wrong, I was well aware that I had a right to

grieve and could be excused for feeling sorry for myself, even if that took me down a path I'd rather not have travelled. But I see it like this: if you've got kids, and your child was in trouble then nothing would stop you getting to them, would it? If you could see your kids after a lengthy absence, nothing would get in your way, would it?

And just because Azaylia had passed, it didn't stop me being a devoted father on a path to seeing her again. So nothing was going to stop me. The difference is that mine isn't a twenty-minute drive. It's a lot tougher, and will probably take me the rest of my life.

So I kicked the booze into touch. No, not completely. I'm not going to sit here and say that I'm teetotal now, because it's not like I was a raging alcoholic in the first place. Certainly I have a drink now and then. But the change is that during the time I'm talking about, I had no functionality. I wasn't active. I wasn't positive. I wasn't having any impact and I definitely wasn't staying true to the promises that I made to myself and to my daughter. I was just feeling sorry for myself. And that's no good to anyone.

So I put the bottle down and picked up a new sense of belief, purpose and destiny.

The Azaylia Foundation had launched on 31 August 2021 and soon after, I was taking part in the first of the challenges that would serve a dual purpose in helping the Foundation: firstly, raising money; secondly, providing publicity and raising awareness.

The first challenge fulfilled that remit entirely. It took place in September 2021 and involved myself, Matty and Tamika biking 1,040 miles from Land's End to John O'Groats.

Leading up to this, my coping mechanism involved getting outside. I knew that Azaylia was in the sky, looking down on me. I believed that when I was outside, she could hear me, see me, follow me and be with me. And after all, the pledge was to take her to places, so outside was where I needed to be. Running, cycling, swimming – these things have saved my life because they gave me a further focus. They gave me a purpose, a reason to be outside and be with her. My lens was changing. I was changing, because I was looking up to the sky, appreciating the air, the grass, everything I would see in nature. Things that I had never really seen – as in *properly seen* – before, now I was seeing for the very first time, and in the most beautiful and vibrant colours, as if the world was coming alive to me. I felt like a caterpillar becoming a butterfly – a creature shedding its skin but taking on another form.

I'd run. I didn't know my distance. I didn't know my time. I just used to run and run, like Forrest Gump.

If everybody in my town didn't know me before, then they knew me now, because I was outside running (and sorry if during that time you wanted to stand and chat and I just ran past. I meant no rudeness by it, it's just that I just needed to keep going).

Matty, my brother, was like, 'I want to run.'

My cousin Tamika – Miks – that absolute legend, said, 'I want to run.'

So now we were three Forrest Gumps running together. So now we were thinking, *What's an amazing journey that we can embark upon? Doesn't have to be running, could be cycling.*

The furthest point south to the furthest point north of Great Britain – Land's End to John O'Groats. Let's do it.

Nobody ever said it would be easy, least of all me. But although I give so much during these challenges, and I know that by appearing on TV I keep my daughter's name in the light (and I always, always represent the colour orange), I take something from it as well, because doing what I do gives me solace; it helps me to understand and process my grief. I know that by taking action, I am honouring her. I'm honouring the name of Azaylia and paying tribute to her bravery by showing mental and physical courage of my own. I always say that she taught me so much, and she continues to do so by providing me with a guiding light, by being a beacon of hope that shows me a pathway through the hardship.

You could say that it was by throwing down a gauntlet for myself that I had a reason to turn my back on the bottle, to get out of bed, pull on my trainers and hit the road. Sure, you could say that. But I know different: I know that she threw down the gauntlet for me.

CHAPTER 51

Were we capable? Probably not.

Had we trained enough? Hm, probably not.

I'm a ninety-six kilos guy. This is the funny thing about some of these Ultra Challenges. Same with the 100 miles in twenty-four hours. I just do not have an ultra-athlete build. I'm strength and speed, not endurance.

We got in touch with a few people who'd cycled it before, a gentleman called Tom who helped source our bikes and plan routes, and a lady called Jess who helped us out with our training. Loads of people were telling us, 'No, no, you've never cycled this distance before. You haven't trained enough. Maybe you should do a relay.'

We were like, 'No, we got this.'

And I'm so glad we did, because it really was an incredible, electric experience.

The unexpected joy began at Land's End, where well-wishers came out in force, wearing orange and chanting, 'Let's go, Champ.'

We had published the expected checkpoint arrival times on Instagram, but were still as surprised as we were overjoyed to see the turnout at every stage. There would be hundreds of people sometimes: orange tops, teddy bears, drawings, placards. The love and compassion in their hearts was a sight to behold.

I tried to speak to everyone. I wanted to get hugs from everyone (I'd become a big hug person – *big* hug person) because with the exception of Azaylia's Day, and I suppose to a slightly lesser extent the day of the big clap, I had never actually witnessed in flesh and blood and in three dimensions the support that was out there for Azaylia.

Besides which, the clap and Azaylia's Day were events that brought the local community out of doors. Now we were talking about supporters from literally up and down the length of the country.

I knew they were out there, of course. The fact that we'd raised £1.6m on a GoFundMe appeal told me that. Just that previously they'd been pixels on a computer screen. Now they were here, out of doors and in person.

It choked me up, it really did. Like I say, I was appreciating life now. I'll give you an example. Before, I'd never really appreciated the water, the grandeur of the sea in particular. But during the ride whatever time of morning or night, if I saw the sea, I'd have to get in. I was finding that being in the water gave me a kind of cold water therapy that helped centralise me. It gave me a connection to the present, and because it felt so elemental, it gave me a connection to Azaylia. She was no longer solely in the sky; she was in the water too.

In Bristol there must have been thousands of people there

to greet us as we cycled into the city. Everyone roaring, every-one cheering.

That day I was probably the most tired I had ever been up until that point in my life, but I stayed behind for four and a half hours, just to speak to as many people as I could. Everyone had a gift for us. Everyone had a story about their memories of Azaylia, how her journey had inspired them; in some cases how reading about Azaylia had saved their lives, relationships and so on.

It was the same at Stratford-upon-Avon. Hundreds of people there. We arrived in Nottingham at midnight and all we could see was hundreds of phone lights as we approached the checkpoint.

The ride went on to raise over £100,000 for the Foundation, and that, if nothing else, made me realise that this journey could help so many other people – that the love for Azaylia could help them too. What a positive effect she was having. What good she was already doing in this world. We saw that behind us was a pride of lions who could push to make a difference for kids who really needed it and help continue this amazing legacy.

I also realised that I needed the boost from my family and the community to keep me on my path. It's they who help me to inspire and motivate people who go through mental health struggles; it's they who inspire me to make a difference in the childhood cancer space. All of it is powered by the community.

When we had finished the Land's End to John O'Groats bike ride it was of course still World Childhood Cancer Awareness Month, and so we wanted to continue with our fundraising efforts. How? By doing the Three Peaks Challenge, with a 700-mile cycle between each mountain, which involved climbing Ben Nevis then Scafell Pike and then Snowdon.

In all that month, we cycled over 1,800 miles and climbed the three hardest mountains in the UK. Not bad to kick off the Foundation. Then on Christmas Day, I ran a marathon in order to raise money for a young cancer sufferer named Alexander. The following April, we did the ultramarathon, the one which ended in Trafalgar Square.

They say it takes three months to recover from a 100-mile run. Me, I had just two weeks before I had to go and film *SAS: Who Dares Wins*; after that, I filmed the show *Go Hard or Go Home* for the BBC.

Nobody ever said it would be easy. Least of all me.

CHAPTER 52

Go Hard or Go Home kicked off with a call from my manager, asking if I was interested in a new show, which at that point was called *Warrior Island*. The idea was that a bunch of 'warriors' – me being one of them – would be mentoring people in their twenties who had all been through something difficult in their lives.

It wasn't the most money I've been offered for TV. It wasn't going to be a guaranteed big show like *SAS: Who Dares Wins*, but even so, it was a quick decision because I fell in love with the concept, which was absolutely in tune with where I am in my life right now.

The thing is, I can put videos on the internet, and people will tell me that they find them inspiring, and it's great to get that feedback. But at the end of the day, how do I really know? How can I actually see if what I'm doing has an effect?

This was an opportunity to be with a person, and see how

much I could change their life. All I was told at that point was that my trainee would not only need help with their physical fitness, but would have been through something in their life that had affected their mental health as well.

That really interested me, because having been through it myself, I feel like I have a voice to speak to people who've come from where I come from in terms of trauma and loss, in terms of knowing how low you can go, and what you have to do to drag yourself up from that.

It was six weeks in the Dominican Republic, and you might find this difficult to believe, but I knew that was going to be difficult for me. Not only was I fatigued after the challenges, but it meant I couldn't visit my daughter's resting place. So that was a wrench. Also, I do the things that I do every day – running, kayaking, cycling, training – to keep myself sane and grounded and hungry and pushing myself forward.

SAS was two weeks. This was six. It was close to the year's anniversary of Azaylia's passing. So that was difficult, too.

On the plus side, I'd have the chance to help someone with their pain and trauma. Coach them into physical fitness, counsel them into a better mental space.

We had to choose our colours. The one thing that was non-negotiable for me was that I had be orange. Next, it was up to the trainees to choose their own warrior, and mine was a fantastic guy called Dylan Spaull, who had fought and beaten testicular cancer. What I quickly realised about twenty-three-year-old Dylan was that he was a nice guy, and even though he was a really positive influence for the group, he had no real belief in himself.

If you've seen the show, you'll know the idea was for

warriors to coach their trainees through various challenges. With Dylan, I decided to train and mentor him the same way that I trained and mentored myself, and that began with finding out why he was on the show. Genuinely, I knew nothing about him up until that moment.

And it was the maddest thing. What an example of how much my life has changed. Number one, I find myself on a little island in the Dominican Republic, sitting next to a guy telling me a story of how he'd faced death. It was a story that brought me to tears, that made me put my arm around him, because I wanted him to feel strength and love and know that he wasn't going to break down while he was telling me this story.

All the other contestants were phoning home, but Dylan didn't want to do that. He explained that he didn't want to talk to his mum because she treated him like a piece of glass and was always too protective of him.

That's when I had to explain to him my story, how I'd had a child with cancer, how I would have done anything to take that cancer away from my daughter. And how I knew that his mum would have felt the same. And she would do anything in her power now to make sure that doesn't happen again.

'But I ain't your mum,' I told him, 'And if you want people to stop treating you like a piece of glass then it's time to act like a piece of steel.'

Again, it was mad. Having had testicular cancer, Dylan only has one ball. And if you've read this far, you'll know that I'm the same. I knew how I felt about having one ball. It's embarrassing; you don't want anyone to know about it. But the fact of the matter is that Dylan believed his cancer defined him, and I needed to make him realise that it doesn't.

I thought, *If I tell him, everybody is going to know I only have one ball. But do you know what? I don't care.* How this guy felt about himself meant more to me than what anybody would think about me. I just wanted to make him feel comfortable, not alone. Having one ball, it's not going to define you. Look at me, look at what I'm capable of. So I did. I told him. And this was another way that I'd changed. No way would I have told him that before. And no way would I have done so on camera.

Once I'd found out Dylan's background, I assured him that I'd get him to where he wanted to go, saying to him, 'The only thing I ask from you is that you have to believe in yourself, because I can't believe in you more than you believe in yourself, and I won't ask you to do anything that I'm not prepared to do myself.'

I made it a point of doing all the forms of training with him. Every session I did with him was training as well as counselling; it was explaining *why* I do this, *how* it was going to benefit him, putting life into perspective for him.

And to be fair to him, I couldn't have asked for a better trainee. He was like a sponge soaking up every piece of information. All the tough love I gave him – all the strength, courage, resilience and tenacity. He absorbed it, he implemented it into his time on the island and he is still implementing it now into his life.

Hopefully this isn't a spoiler, but Dylan won. And what a deserving winner he was. Not only was he the trainee who was the most transformed, but he was also the trainee who put in the greatest amount of work. I still speak to him every week, make sure that I check in on him. He sends me his training, letting me know how he's doing. I spoke to his mum the other day, she couldn't thank me enough.

I felt like I was a warrior to some of the other trainees as well, in particular Seb, another of the trainees who had been struggling with his grief after the death of his mum. Seb has been struggling recently. He sent me a long message the other day because it was coming up to his mum's birthday and he didn't know how to handle it. He felt like he'd lost himself a bit since coming off the show and that he wasn't capable of dealing with the situation.

I was actually at my daughter's resting place at the time so I asked for his number, called him, and sat on the phone with him for an hour or so, talking him through how I handle the big occasions. The birthdays. The anniversaries.

How I challenge myself.

I knew he that he had been training to run a 10k for charity so I said to Seb, 'Have you run 10k yet?'

He said, 'Nah, not yet, mate,' in his broad Bolton accent.

'When it's your mum's birthday, I want you to go out and run 10k. I want you to get up early rather than let the day dawn on you. I want you to go and attack that day. Because by running the furthest you've ever run on your mum's birthday, you will be able to use the pain of missing her to push yourself to a new level and achieve something you've never achieved before. You'll have made yourself proud and you would have made your mum proud. And you know that every step you take, she's watching you. And when you're finished, you can look up to the sky and know that you did it because of her.'

He did it. And then he posted about it on Instagram and gave me a nice little namecheck.

'Honestly, I'm buzzing,' he said, which was very Seb. By doing this first 10k, making himself leave the house and use the grief he was feeling to push him forward, suddenly the charity run became an achievable target.

That show was brilliant for me because I knew that my part in it was to make Dylan realise how strong he actually was. He was already amazing. He was already incredible. He was already strong. My job was to bring that out, apply that bit of pressure, give him that tough love and get him to step outside of his comfort zone so he realised what he was capable of. And it was great to go through that on the show because it gave me confirmation that what I'm doing is worthwhile. Me being here is worthwhile. I love what I do on social media, but that's just words on a screen. When you actually get somebody there and you can see the effect that your words and deeds are having, that's something really special.

All the times I've been on TV before it was about furthering my career or getting more exposure. I did *SAS* to throw myself into the deep end, to see if I was capable enough to be the person I wanted to be at my most vulnerable point. But this show was different in that it fitted in with everything that I was trying to do with my life and still am right now. It reflected the difference in me. Everything before my daughter was about me. But now my life is about how I can affect, influence and evoke positivity in others, and this was a great opportunity for me to do that.

It was a refreshing show too. Something different from the usual diet. The response I've had has been amazing. People got to see how for young people who are not necessarily into fitness, having a positive, not-quitting attitude and integrating fitness into their lives can really turn things around. These days it seems like every man and his dog has mental health issues, which in one sense is great, because it means that more people are talking about it, but it's also apparent to me that not all those people want to do something about their problems. They like talking about them, but don't feel able to tackle them. So this show was great in that it illustrated that with a bit of positivity, some tough love, a goal, a target, an ambition and self-belief, you can achieve a stronger, more capable version of yourself. It's a show that actually helped those who watched, and you can't really say that about a lot of TV shows.

CHAPTER 53

I think of Azaylia as being with me now, because one thing I know is that I will never stop being her father. That's how I still class myself and always will.

And you might call me crazy, but I still talk as if she's here. In so many ways she remains very present in my life.

Of course I have the beautiful but occasionally harsh reminder of my brother's little girl, Anaya. She's now running around and talking, and when I see her, I wonder, would you, Azaylia, be doing that? Would you be doing the same? Would you look the same? Would you sound the same?

Something I think about all the time. What sort of person would she have turned out to be, if she had lived? Well, I'm sure we would have been best mates. She had a bit of Grandad Cain in her. You could tell she was going to be cheeky and probably wouldn't take no for an answer. But she would have been a courteous little girl. Saf would have been stricter than me, because I'm quite laidback, but even so, I'm all about good manners. If you've got good manners and if you've got respect, I can work with that.

I was already picturing the days when I would ring the school and tell them Azaylia was poorly, and then say to her, 'Where do you want to go today? Don't tell your mum.'

She was a daddy's girl and always would be. I knew that because we were best friends, even when she was a baby; our connection couldn't be denied. That's how it always was and how it always would be. She and I were going to be as thick as thieves.

Whatever her journey in life, and whatever jams she found herself in, I had decided that I would always be calm and non-judgemental, because if you go in all guns blazing, that's when you push people away. I'd be approachable. If anything needed to be sorted out, I'd sort it out, but I'd give her the opportunity to do it first, so that she could learn. Either way, she would know that I had her back; that she could come to me when she needed support or a shoulder to cry on.

Boyfriends! God. I can imagine that I would have said, 'Treat her with respect, have manners. If you make her cry or play away, maybe that's up to you two to sort out. But if you ever lay your hands on her, then we got a problem.'

People say to me, 'But Ashley, you've thought about all of this stuff. You're such a great dad to Azaylia, you're clearly cut out to be a father ...'

What about having another child?

No doubt. A lot of people say that. And it's true that I think I was made to be a dad. For all the gifts that the good Lord gave me, the best one was the ability to be a father. I connect with children. They connect with me. If I'm around a child, I'll give that kid all of my attention for that time. I don't let them run riot and I make sure they say their please and thank yous, I make sure they have respect. In return they get my attention and they get my time.

But another child? That's another question, isn't it? I mean, Saf and I originally planned to have a few. I wanted five or six kids. The idea was for Azaylia to be the first of an amazing family. And it's funny because right from the start, I always detected that proper big-sister vibe in her. I was also thinking that one day her little brothers and sisters would find out about her fight against cancer, and they'd be completely in awe of her; they'd know how strong she was. As a result their big sister would be their hero and protector, and because she'd been through so much, she wouldn't let anything go wrong for them.

But the answer is no – no, I don't see myself having another child. And the reason is that right now I couldn't love another child the way I loved Azaylia, and maybe more importantly, the way I still *do* love Azaylia. And that's just not fair on a new arrival. I haven't moved on.

Then of course there's the fact that Saf and I are no longer together. Like I say, we're still very close, and our work as trustees of the Foundation means that we remain in close contact, but to a certain extent we've gone on different paths. Right now I'm trying to impact the world, trying to make the world a better place, and that means that I don't even have time for myself, let alone for a romantic relationship. To be honest, I've never been so driven in my life. I've never *achieved* so much in my life. I've never helped so many people. The sheer amount of drive I have – it doesn't really leave room for anybody else.

I ask myself, what has changed me more? Becoming a father to Azaylia or losing Azaylia? The answer is that it is the journey. Obviously the passing of my daughter has had more of an impact on my life than the birth because of the extreme trauma of it, and if Azaylia was in this world now, and I was her daddy, I wouldn't be pushing myself the way I am.

But even so, it was the journey. Not the birth. Not her passing. It was the between part that changed me as a person, because even if Azaylia had survived the cancer, the Foundation would still be here. And if I had Azaylia now, I believe that I would still be an advocate for mental health, and for childhood cancer, and I would still fly a flag for hope, for optimism, for seeing a light at the end of the tunnel.

That was her gift to me.

CHAPTER 54

In August 2022, we completed a five-marathon challenge, which began in Dublin, and then moved to Belfast, Glasgow and Cardiff before ending up in London. Then in September 2022, we took part in the London-to-Rome cycling challenge, cycling from London to Paris then on to Geneva, before crossing the Alps into Italy and arriving in Rome mid-September.

The London-to-Rome cycling challenge gave me even more time to think about my new philosophy of appreciating and experiencing the world outside. With Azaylia on my shoulder, I was goggle-eyed in wonder at what a beautiful and magical place the world is.

I had so much opportunity to appreciate it. When you're cycling or running, you're churning away for up to ten hours a day, and you have to spend time inside yourself. During these hours, you see beauty. You see different parts of the world, and how awesome it is.

I'd be thinking, this is where I'm taking her, to see all this wonderful stuff, and not only am I taking her with me, but every day, we're raising awareness, raising money. Every day, people are looking at us and thinking, *If these motherfuckers can cycle into the Alps then I can go to the gym and do an hour.* One minute we were in Trafalgar Square, the next we're under the Eiffel Tower, and we've cycled there. You wouldn't drive it, yet we've *cycled* it.

The next minute we're in Switzerland, Lake Geneva. We're at the bottom of the Alps and climbing. Some of the climbs were four and a half hours long, and you can't get off, because you've got clip-ins so if you stop, you can't get going again. You have to keep on going. You climb and you climb. You get a little bit of flat and then you're climbing again. You look down and see a 6,000-foot drop. You get to the top, you look at the signs and you climbed 11,000 feet. You're crossing the border at 11,000 feet in the air from France to Italy. You get to the end and go to see the leaning Tower of Pisa and then in Rome the Coliseum.

And that's where we finished, because I believe that Azaylia's a gladiator, a warrior. I believe that all these kids fighting cancer are gladiators and warriors. I remember sitting there at the end, thinking, *I cycled this for my daughter – with my daughter – to help people in this world, and there is no greater feeling that I could have in this world right now, apart from if she was here.*

You might wonder, then, if I do what I do for selfish reasons, given that I have this experience. I can't deny that it gives me something as well. It gives me healing and fulfilment. I know that I'm not getting up every morning and looking forward to a whisky that night and wondering what's on the telly. I'm getting up every morning and I'm choosing to *do* something with my life. I'm doing it for that reason.

After London-to-Rome came the London Marathon in October. By the time I reached London, I was physically and mentally exhausted, and although I won't go into it here, it was a very low time. Dark thoughts. Suicidal thoughts. I was pulled back from the brink. Literally pulled back from the brink (and you know who you are, the person responsible) in order to keep on fighting.

I suppose that I had a bit of a nervous breakdown, and it might sound crazy now, but I kind of needed it: it was necessary, because I gained the experience to talk about it. I gained the self-knowledge to know that the path of self-destruction is never the right one.

Would I have reached heaven if I'd kept on drinking or, worse, taken my own life? Almost certainly not. At the end of the year I did my Christmas bike ride to raise money for two children, Elaiya and Philo. I also went abroad to achieve my skydiving licence, something I've been wanting to do for two reasons: firstly because it meant facing up to one of my biggest fears, that of heights, and knowing I could only do it with the strength Azaylia gave me; knowing she was watching over me and would protect me until the day she needs me back. And secondly, because I wanted to be in the sky with her – to tell her I loved her from the highest point a freefalling human can be.

In all, we finished 2022 with some pretty impressive stats. We had raised over £200,000 and made donations of more than £700,000. These included new research donations to Oxford

University, Great Ormond Street Hospital and the University of Birmingham and Birmingham Children's Hospital, and eight individual-treatment donations for Lee, Rudi, Aaron, Jayden, Yuvraj, Ethan, Elaiya and Philo.

We had also launched a ground-breaking PhD fund, to fund the next generation of leaders in childhood cancer, and introduced our first community powered awareness and fund-raising campaign, 'Wear Orange for Azaylia', with over 100 schools participating.

CHAPTER 55

What we have achieved is awesome. What's more, there's no real sign of it dropping off. The support's remained absolutely incredible.

That support keeps my fires lit. Yeah, I have my down days and my low nights. If you look at my Instagram you'll see those times when I've been very low, and I've had to drive somewhere, park up and scroll through music and videos just to remind myself of Azaylia, shed a few tears and say a few words to her.

On one occasion recently, I paid a visit to my dad, who was able to give me some wise words. My dad is just one of the people around me who helps keep me going. If you're in my team and you're reading this, thank you. Thank you from the bottom of my heart. Me, I was chosen for this life, and all glory goes to Azaylia, an angel who selected me for this purpose, but for those around me, it's different. They made a *choice*. They have *chosen* to be a part of it. And that's what makes them so important, so vital. I know what I'm heading for. I know that my validation will come at the end of my journey. I hope the same for them.

Meanwhile, the challenge show goes on. At the time of writing, I'm in training for a 125-mile, 24-hour kayak race along the Thames from Devizes to Westminster in April 2023. At the end of that month I'm running the London Marathon again, then taking part in Ride London. And then in July, it's the big one: the Yukon 1000.

The way that began was that I had a message from Georgia Harrison, basically telling me about her former personal trainer, Gaz Johnson, who had completed a lot of extreme Ultra Challenges, events in the Arctic, Brazil and so on. Gaz wanted to take part in an annual challenge called the Yukon 1000, had never managed to get a place and now needed a partner for his latest attempt. Georgia knew his mindset. She knows my mindset. She thought we should speak. So I said, 'Yeah, call, let's have a chat.'

We spoke. These days, now that I know him, I know how to deal with him. But my first impression was, *This guy is crazy*. And he is. He's absolutely nuts. I was thinking, *If I do this challenge then I've got to spend ten days with this guy. Do I want to do that?* I wasn't even thinking about the dangers of the challenge itself – didn't even know them yet – I was just wondering if I could spend almost two weeks with this guy.

However, having spent time with Gaz, I know that he's a really nice and honourable guy who also had a daughter with leukemia so this opportunity just feels right. So I agreed to it.

And still I knew hardly anything about it. But the reason I agreed was because after Azaylia passed, I was struggling, as you know. I'd started running, and I ran and I ran, until one day I got on my knees and spoke to God. I said, 'God, I don't know what more I can do, but I'm ready.'

I wanted to show Him that I was ready to do anything – to sacrifice *everything* – in order to fulfil my promise of taking Azaylia around the world. So I said yes to the Yukon challenge, and the reason I said yes was because I'd asked God for an opportunity to do this for her. And I'd asked Him for an opportunity to help motivate and inspire people, and here it was. So if you think about it, it doesn't matter how tough it is, it doesn't matter how dangerous it is; it doesn't matter if I come back or not. When would I otherwise have the opportunity to take my daughter from Canada, in to the Arctic Circle and then to Alaska? I asked God for an opportunity, He gave it to me, so I'm doing it.

I remember taking a Zoom call with the race organiser and him sitting there, an ex-special forces guy. I felt my stomach churn as he told us all about it, because up until then I really didn't know the ins and outs of the race. He was saying, 'Gary, I know you've been in the military. Ash, I know you done Ultra Challenges, but this is the real deal.'

The challenge, he told us, involves kayaking 1,000 miles from Canada to the Arctic Circle to Alaska. You kayak for eighteen hours a day with no support, no assistance. You then have an hour to pitch your tent. You can't eat where you sleep in case of grizzly bears, so you have to walk a kilometre from your tent just to eat. Then you get four or five hours' sleep before embarking on eighteen hours of kayaking again.

It's the world's toughest survival endurance race and the longest kayak race in the world. There are fatalities.

'This race is completely unsupported,' he continued. 'You don't get help. If your boat capsizes, no one is going be there to save you. If you get hypothermia, we probably won't reach you for two days. You're going to be in grizzly bear territory, and there's not much you can do if a grizzly bear attacks you. You need to know what you're getting yourself into.'

I feel like in life there is always a test for what you say you want. If you ask God, or whatever higher power you believe in, for strength, you won't just be handed strength, instead you'll get an *opportunity* to be strong. If you ask for courage, you won't be given bravery, you will be given the chance to be courageous.

After that call, I was thinking, *This is a test. This is like, well, if fulfilling your journey really means more to you than life itself, the fear of death can't be enough to stop you.*

And it doesn't. I believe that I will be protected until the day that Azaylia needs me back. And I don't let difficulty stop me. I don't let risk stop me. Our time is not promised on this Earth. I think that if I go out there and don't come back, then it's my time.

And if I go out there and come back, then great, what's next?

Obviously we've been training like absolute warriors. I have a machine called a kayaking ergometer that I've been using to build up my strength, added to which we've been kayaking on rivers, day and night.

For the 125-mile Thames race we'll be using a bigger-than-usual boat. It'll be orange, of course, but larger because there was no point in competing using one of the paper-thin kayaks if it's not the sort of boat we'd be using on the Yukon challenge. You can't do it in an ordinary kayak. So it's tough, but it's necessary.

Embarking on these challenges, I think about the fact that I quit *SAS: Who Dares Wins*. The thing is, I really should have won that show. I believe I was the best, but I quit during the interrogation. I tore off my armband indicating that I wanted to retire, thinking, *I really don't need this mental torture in my life. I've had enough of that, it's only a show.* But I shouldn't have done, and I look back with regret about that.

Still, I learned from it. And because of that experience I now go into things thinking, *I'm never going to quit again.* I don't want that feeling in my world. That feeling of regret at having quit. Kayaking is going to be physically uncomfortable, it's going to be cold, wet, filthy, painful and incredibly dangerous, but I believe that the weight of pain is temporary while the price of regret lasts forever. And because of that, I know I won't quit.

The whole challenge experience has changed me, of course, beyond all recognition. I've had to become a different person in order to do what I do. A person who is more aware of the world around him, more conscious. I haven't stopped moving forward – that remains a part of me – but I'm still able to take the time and look around, and nowadays I know that I could sit in the wilderness for hours and appreciate the trees, the grass, the sky, just as easily as I could be in a club and lose myself in the music. I've no longer got half an eye on what's around the corner.

People talk about happiness. But is there any such thing? When my daughter was diagnosed with cancer and then passed away, it took the dream of happiness out of my life. The illusion was removed, and I started to realise that for me, just as it is for many people, there is no such thing as happiness. And then I thought, *If there's no such thing for some people, why would there be such a thing for everybody?* and I started to understand myself. I began to really feel every second. I realised that although there are happy moments, happy memories and happy times, there's no such thing as a straight uninterrupted line of it. So I don't have happiness and by that standard, never will. But that's because I seek something more important, which is fulfillment, and to me that's worth more than happiness.

My first action each morning is to look at a picture of Azaylia. I look at the picture and the next thing I do is remember the best moments of my life, which were waking up in the hospital, opening my eyes and seeing that smile on her face. It was the most incredible time, a time that even managed to compensate for the terror of the nights, knowing that she had a smile on her face and that we had another day together, and how we'd get the blinds open, get the music on, dance and make the most of our time together.

I can't help it, but I get to thinking something else as well. I'll remember that she's no longer there. The thought comes that *I haven't got you any more, I can't see you any more, there was nothing I could do to stop you passing.* And even though I take so much comfort from the fact that she lost her life and passed lying in mine and her mother's arms, and that she would have wanted it that way, being with the people she loved the most, I can't prevent that loss hitting me like a ton of bricks. I can do nothing about a thought that really troubles me, which is that she was alone on her journey to the other side. It's the biggest journey you will ever make in this life. And not only did she have to undertake her journey before me, but she didn't have me on the other side to wait for her. Parents guide their children through childhood. The child falls down and bangs their knee, and you pick them up and kiss it better. You tell them that it's not so bad. You're there for them.

But that journey – that final journey that she had to make – she had to make it alone, which haunts me.

So all I can do now is hope that I make her proud, which I do by helping to create a brighter future for children with cancer, and by motivating, helping and inspiring people with mental health issues to believe that they can overcome their difficulties.

Even so, I know that no matter how much I do, at the end of it, I'm still empty-handed. Not in terms of finance, success or credibility, but empty-handed that she's still not here, and that's one of the hardest things to get my head around. It dawns on me afresh every day. I have that moment of knowing.

I guess this is where strength comes in. I can't start my day with bitterness or hold hate in my heart when all I wish to do is show love for this world and the people in it, and that's as a result of the purest love that I was privileged enough to have been given by my daughter.

It's an effort of will sometimes to bring myself up. I know that the pain never leaves my eyes. It's something everybody says about me: 'I can see the pain in your eyes.' They wonder if I should see a grief counsellor. But the problem is that unless somebody has been through the experience that I have, then I'm sorry, but they're not qualified to be able to help me. I also think that I've achieved a huge amount without a counsellor.

If I'd gone to counselling and achieved what I've achieved, you'd get that counsellor a Christmas present, wouldn't you? You'd say, 'Ash, you've done really well, you should keep going.' So what's the reason why you think I need to go to counselling? The counsellor might specialise in loss, but have they lost a child? Probably not. Has the counsellor lost a child and then completed a bunch of Ultra Challenges? Almost definitely not. Has the counsellor started a movement to tackle childhood cancer even through relentless amounts of hate, negativity and bitterness? Almost definitely not.

So how are they going to know how to advise me?

Maybe I could have done with a counsellor before, but for the first time in my life I know who I am and where I'm going, and I don't really want to change that. I've been given my purpose, so I don't need an outside influence in my life. Most of the time I feel strong and in those times when I falter I have people around to reach out to.

A lot of those people who advise me to go to counselling struggle to get out of bed in the morning. I don't.

Azaylia gave me purpose.

CHAPTER 56

Here's a funny thing. Apart from the obvious, I don't wish my life had been different. I wouldn't want to change anything that would change my time with Azaylia, and anyway, there's one thing for sure: no decision that I or anybody else took would have made a difference to Azaylia's passing and joining heaven. It was God's will. Everything in my life led to that, and I'm so grateful I had those eight months with her. During that time, I felt like the luckiest man in the world. It was, and still is, an honour to be able to call myself Azaylia's father.

What happened cannot be changed, so now I feel empowered by it. The fact that I'm taking action, that my purpose has given me the strength, resilience, courage and tenacity to be able to do what I have to do now.

I think back on my old life and know that whether I've been lucky or not, the difference is that I had no purpose and no direction before Azaylia. I look at my life today, and I know that even with all the pain and trauma, I would prefer to be the person I am now than the one I was then, because now I am on a more divine path, I see a purposeful way before me. I see a way in which I can affect the world.

Before, I was unconscious to the world, now I am conscious of it. Before, there was no end. There was no goal to my journey. Now I have a goal. Take the example of a spoilt kid who gets everything they want. They don't have to work. They get what they want straight away, they get it now, and as a result they don't place any value on it. They don't know what it took to get it. They just go, 'Wow, I want a new one. I want another one.'

Then you take a kid who's come from nothing, who because they know how hard their mum or dad have worked for the gift really appreciate it.

Me, I feel like that spoilt kid was me before Azaylia, but now I'm changed. Now I look forward to getting to where I'm going, and I know that it will mean so very much more because the journey was hard.

In terms of luck, I've been tested. I've been tested over and over. No doubt about it, my hard times have called on me to dig deep and be a certain kind of person, withstand misfortune and show a bit of grit. But they're tests I feel I've passed and will continue to pass, and that's why I think they're going to let me into heaven. So that one day I'll close my eyes, everything will go black, and then when I open them again, I will have my ultimate prize, because she will be there, waiting to welcome me.

And I will see that smile again.

ACKNOWLEDGEMENTS

These acknowledgements were so hard to write because I worried that I'd leave someone out or forget someone important. And everyone that has been a part of my life or on this journey with me is important. It's almost impossible to properly thank every single person – my mum, my dad, my brothers and sisters, my aunties and uncles, my grandparents, my cousins, all my family, I am eternally grateful for having you in my life; to my friends who have stood by me through thick and thin; to Saf, who gave me the most incredible gift I could have hoped, wished or dreamed for in Azaylia; to the nurses and doctors and hospital staff who helped to care for Azaylia and all the people who donated their time and signed up for the bone marrow register; to everyone at The Azaylia Foundation and everyone who raises money for it; to everyone involved in the challenges I do, that's come along to cheer me and the team on, or helped organise them, or sent messages, or just supported me online; to my management, to my book publishers, to absolutely everyone. Please know that you and your support are so appreciated and valued, and always will be. I always said that this journey is inspired by Azaylia but it's really powered by the community, Azaylia's very own pride of lions.

The most important person I want to thank is Azaylia. She is my reason for living. My purpose in life. My angel.

Daddy loves you. I hope and pray that I make you proud. This is for you and I'll never stop fighting.

Until I see you again, baby... x

THE AZAYLIA FOUNDATION

Childhood cancer is the number one killer of children in the UK, yet it receives less than 3 per cent of cancer research funding.

This has drastic implications on early diagnosis, on the availability of new research and new treatments specifically developed for children, on the permanent physical and emotional damage effects from receiving adult treatments, on the availability of new, specialised talent.

The Azaylia Foundation is dedicated to changing a system that has been underfunding childhood cancer for too long. By working with a large community of supporters and a public audience, we:

Raise funds which can be used to fund new research and new talent across prevention, early diagnosis and the availability of new treatments for childhood cancer

Build a movement that demands change through awareness raising and calls to action

Support children accepted into treatment not freely available from the NHS with a donation of up to £10,000

To donate to
THE AZAYLIA FOUNDATION,
please visit
https://theazayliafoundation.com/donate
or scan this QR code